BUSINESS LEADERSHIP AND SUCCESS

Published by Gilford Publishing, LLC
Library of Congress Catalog Card Number: 2012901647
CreateSpace, North Charleston, SC
ISBN-10: 1466361069
ISBN-13: 9781466361065

Visit our website at www.veragilford.com

Other books by this author:

Secrets to Losing Weight & Better Health
ISBN 978-0-9704081-0-5
E-book ISBN 978-0-9704081-1-2
Library of Congress Card Catalogue Number
2016901511
Gilford Publishing LLC Miami, FL

Growing Fearless
ISBN/EAN-13: 1492823775/9781492823773
Library of Congress Card Catalogue Number: 2013920040

Special quantity discounts for bulk purchases available for sales promotions. For details contact the publisher, P.O. Box 12553, Miami, FL 33101 or email: Vera@VeraGilford.com

Table of Contents

Introduction

This book is a guide, like the map of a golf course to steer you along your journey. It highlights the beauty of business that points toward success, but also prepares you for obstacles, blind spots, and challenges that threaten to keep you from experiencing your full business and leadership potential. .This book helps you create excellent quality in your products and services. It helps you profit in your business and succeed in your leadership pursuits.

One key to success in business is to find what you genuinely love, unlock your potential and pursue it. When you find your passion, and merge it with a satisfying and meaningful purpose, it helps you live healthier, happier and produce greater wealth.

LINK # 1

THE CROSSSROAD TO
A MEANINGFUL PURSUIT

"If you find the point where your mother's path crosses your father's path you will find your purpose in life."

Hearing that intrigued me, so I set out to find that crossroad. When I started my journey I had successfully finished law school, passed the bar exam, practiced law, been published in several publications, partnered in several business ventures and visited five of the seven continents. Little did I know that this quest would be unlike any other venture. It would take me into the unknown.

When you go on a quest you are looking for something that you hope or expect to find. You do not know how significantly it may change your life.

At the crossroad of my mother and father's path was where his intellectual business principles merged with her spiritual values. My father's soul was dominated by business. My mother took a spiritual path that gave her a similar sense of accomplishment. His desire for business success tested his persistence. Her inner personal values solidified her persistence. His business objectives confronted him with outer competitors in the same way that her inner personal missions confronted

1

her with deep soul-searching challenges. Both had a method to apply discipline to a structured process, however, the "business first," principles he advocated were not exactly consistent with her spiritual, "one way to heaven" rules.

The measure of success for my father's business and my mother's spiritual path boiled down to a few key business and character components. One was the degree to which they found meaning in what they did. The peace my mother found in the church and within quiet chambers of herself, my father found in business and on the golf course.

My deep analysis into inner spaces of my parents took me deep within myself to places I had never been, places only I could go. When you are searching for something it opens up little rooms hidden deep within yourself. No matter how answers come they bring revelations, sometimes only you can understand what meaning they have in your life.

Digging deep within yourself forces hidden emotions and other clutter to surface. This makes you more aware of life's questions like who really thinks your thoughts. You began to see how perfectly life brings experiences to fulfill your deepest thoughts and feelings.

Taking the time to do a thorough assessment in your life and business brings this same awareness to your logical mind. Deep assessments regarding business help you measure your passion and priority for managing people, making decisions and producing money. You gain an appreciation for how much material possessions can satisfy your soul's yearning to succeed.

As you develop expertise about yourself and your chosen field, you obtain answers to your soul's questions. You ultimately discover that in order for money to make you happy, you have to be happy without it. Fulfillment comes from being not having. As you learn to be present with yourself and your environment you become a more successful leader.

A leader's intellectual and emotional intelligence is not measured by money gender or color but by sound thoughts

My father went into business partly to make a difference, but mostly to make money. As he successfully achieved his goals his pride grew. The more successful he became the more his ego grew and took on its own identity. Eventually, it made decisions that the analytical sharp businessman within him would not have made. Like a sheet of ice beneath his feet that started to separate between his right and left foot, the gap widened causing him to have more regrets about actions he had taken. This caused his inner stability to lessen and led him to search more in the outer world for the peace he could not find within.

Miscalculations that leave you with regrets wishing your venture was more in alignment with the real you come from failing to accurately assess your personal and business mission before embarking on your journey. Finding true meaning is a measure of how honest you are in doing your homework before embarking on a path. It also requires flexibility to change your direction if you have a profound discovery that change is needed.

If venturing down a road to pursue what you think is passion turns out to be a miscalculated desire, continuing down that road only protects and keeps a false premise in place. This can be the nucleus from which an "emotional blind spot" begins to form. No matter what you build on top of it the foundation will remain shaky. The emotional mind will nurture and protect a lie behind a fortress that holds it in place. The emotional mind then begins to control your decisions and dominate your actions, while your analytical mind becomes inactive. This keeps your analytical mind dulled while the emotional mind takes charge.

Lurking "blind spots" like these keep the analytical mind from being fully aware. "Don't hold me responsible," becomes the response of the inactive analytical mind.

Blind spots are mostly known while driving a car. Imagine you are driving down the highway about to change lanes. You look in the rear view mirror, then, you look to your side. Nothing appears to be there. Just as you attempt to change lanes a horn signals a warning, there is danger of impact if you continue. No matter how many years you have been driving experience does not prevent blind spots from catching you off guard. Blind spots leave you saying, "I never saw that coming."

Blind spots can also develop in your life or business when your vision is blurred or when you are too attached to the position directly in front of you to see obvious pitfalls a little further ahead. Preventing disaster caused by a blind spot requires quick reflexes to stay the course or maybe change directions from negative to positive thoughts, energy or influences.

Blind spots can keep you from following-up, showing up or going the distance to do what is necessary. Blind spots develop resistance that pulls against your attempt to do anything else. Your longing urges you forward to actively pursue the business, while procrastination pulls you away from doing what it takes for completion. Facing yourself becomes your hardest challenge. This is a mountain that only you can climb. Until you conquer this challenge, you will face this same obstacle and constantly repeat the course.

In business or your personal leadership closed minded decisions may cause a blind spot. The result, when you have not opened your mind to a possible alternative position, is analyzing facts with an ineffective assessment that considers mostly pros that support your position. When you make decisions in a closed state of mind, you simply search for all the reasons to justify your pre-determined outcome. The effectiveness of your outcome will be as accurate as the validity of your analysis.

Blind spots are limitations that can be revealed through a deep assessment. Unfortunately, a deep assessment requires sorting through a disarray of baggage; but in the end it makes you more enlightened.

The anxiety that results from worry resides in a very similar little room of your emotional mind as the joy that comes from passion. It is your choice to have either. The discomfort that often comes with regret makes you want to detour around that little room. This becomes a limitation that sparks imbalance.

When there is imbalance you are not fully in charge. You will never reach your maximum potential. There will always be something that stops you. The little room you want to avoid is the one you most need to visit because it is where you find the key to unlock and resolve hidden secrets that have the power to control your actions.

Imbalance between your emotional and analytical awareness begins to form a mental boulder. Sometime later when you ask yourself, "Why did I do that?" Regret is a signal that the damage is already done. Then it is too late. Imbalance inhibits you and limits your potential to be greater, to climb higher.

Searching for my "connecting point" made other blind spots abundantly clear. What I discovered is that major blind spots cannot be seen with your eyes they must be seen with your consciousness. That may require shifting an entire point of view.

Why merge golf and business

A mutual love of sports helped to diminish my parents' apparent differences. Sports and its principles helped to defuse conflict and helped them collaborate to achieve mutual goals, even when their paths parted with different views.

My search for the point where my mother's inner personal values crossed my father's business principles combined business, personal leadership and involved sports. My pursuit led me deep into the soul of two leaders, a spiritually lead homemaker and a businessman, his business and a golf course.

The golf course was where my father went for tranquility to gain his inner balance after working six days in his business. On the golf course, what I found resembled the real person buried within my father. It was not that "my father was a businessman," but more accurately, that "a businessman was my father." Understanding this distinction provided a clear foundation for my structure. His soul, which held little capacity outside of his business, crossed that of my mother who was a spiritual powerhouse, could balance dynamic energies but had never balanced a checkbook.

Being successful in a small business is much like a game of golf where you align your goals with your target then drive towards your purpose with precision and passion. For each hole on the golf course, a well-manicured landscape, called the fairway, leads straight from the tee towards the flag. Along the way, in business and golf you must manage the pitfalls that affect your performance. Whether you execute with precision depends on many inner personal obstacles or outer business competitors.

Following the map of the golf course at each hole, you anticipate obstacles like the rough, with dense vegetation. Other hazards may be water, or man-made impediments like bunkers or sand traps. Obstacles and hazards hamper your progress because they slow down the club. With less speed, you lose power. Swinging through the rough takes more energy and strength than a stroke from the fairway or the green, where the grass is lowest and the ball easily rolls into the hole.

When a golf ball falls into a hazard special rules apply. Specially designed golf clubs have more slant or loft on the face of the club.

Loft is the angle on the golf club that gets the ball up and out of a hazard. You want to avoid the hazard as much as possible because it may cause penalty strokes to be added to your game. When necessary to recover from a hazard, rather than increasing your power to drive your ball through thick blades of grass, you compensate by using a higher numbered club with more loft to rise above the situation.

In golf another pitfall you encounter is the outer edges of the fairway, called the rough, where the grass is tall, thick and un-manicured. Closer to your destination, bunkers and sand traps have the potential of keeping your ball stuck in a trap. A bunker in golf is a depression that is usually filled with sand. It is an impediment to a golfer's progress. You encounter more hazards as you get closer to your final destination. Here the grass is cut the lowest.

The stroke with a putter appears easy, but subtle curves and slopes along the green are not obvious. Over-exuberance causes your ball to glide pass your intended goal. This adds unfavorable strokes to your game.

A good execution in business requires you to manage pitfalls similar to those on the golf course. In business obstacles to moving forward may be inner or outer challenges. Boards of directors guide the company forward but all members may not want the same thing. This may create a hazard that pulls the business apart. As you approach the final stretch of your strategic plan, decoys in the form of competitors have the potential of getting you caught in an ambush. Some threats are visible; others are blind spots that come unexpectedly. In business these are the most threatening because they catch you unprepared.

When the ego is in charge, the business is not run by an analytical business leader who has studied the angles and slopes. Instead business decisions are led by fleeting emotions. When an ego becomes threatened it can become very fickle.

Your business plan is your road map

Your business plan helps you to consider and determine the feasibility of going into business. Making a detailed and accurate assessment prior to going into business helps you develop a concrete strategic plan that returns precise results. Executing in the right direction with continuous follow-through ultimately yields positive results in business.

Before preparing a business plan and going into business, first make a personal assessment to study the threads in your tapestry. The purpose of the assessment is to know what you are made of, to determine whether you can handle what is required to survive in business.

Exploring your past, including your character, personality, and abilities demonstrates your successes and failures, and the passions that drive you. It paints a portrait of where you have been. Then look at your interest and skills along with your desires and dreams. Next align them with your future goals.

Following my father's path I ventured into business. Although I had not previously been in business, what I had done as a child was to listen to my father talk about his business at the dinner table; the only time we really conversed together. My parents' conversations over meals had the effect of expanding my reality of operating a business beyond my own personal experience. Years later when I started running my business I continued where his dinner conversations had ended. This confirms that children learn just by being in the presence and hearing discussions at the dinner table.

Like a game of golf, I started my business with what I thought was a thorough assessment. Diligently I prepared a feasibility study and business plan. Eliminating as much of the uncertainty of business was helpful to allow me to step into an unknown venture.

Thoroughly preparing a business plan forced me to evaluate my attitudes, values, skills, priorities, fantasies, and future desires. The answers looked good on paper but seemed hypothetical, like preparing a five-year forecast for a bank loan before you have made your first dime.

Initially, it took a leap of faith to even think about doing it, but, I wasted little energy worrying about uncertainties. Instead, I kept leaping forward on faith. Each step helped me to gain more stability to balance my onward momentum. Continually, taking action to execute my goal helped put elements in place to solve new issues that arose each day. Each decision that I made lessened my agitation.

There was little anxiety about failure when I first went into business. If you have never failed before you do not know the real anxiety of failure. Being ignorant to failure was actually a good thing. If I had known the fear of failure it may have created too much caution to proceed.

Operating a successful business was stored somewhere in my DNA long before I opened the business. Deep within my anatomy I found business success nuggets inherited from my father.

I quickly learned different roles and felt comfortable with the daily operations and accountability including: developing policies and procedures consistent with the mission statement; satisfying customer expectations to increase loyalty; ordering the right amount of supplies, verifying quantities, monitoring inventory, placing advertisements, plus selecting and hiring; creating and enforcing the employee manual and monitoring sales to compare them against revenue projections as well as cost of goods sold.

Neither my assessments nor my business decisions seemed to consider anything about my parents. Little did I know just how much my character and decision making was influenced by them.

I discovered new competitors daily. It is easier to handle the hazards you anticipate. My most competitive threat came from one employee whose actions threw me off guard. Developing a team of employees with my mother's integrity standards and good intentions was not something I considered when I first started the business. Despite all my efforts analyzing resumes to pick employees with good business acumen, examining their motives was not a priority at the time.

Considering resumes and spending time to train had left me feeling good about my choices. My company mission and policies were well clarified and communicated. This one employee, however, had a very different game plan. The blind spot I discovered through her is what revealed just how critical the value of my mother's spiritual principles and inner knowing plays in business.

There were two parts of my father. There was the intellectual part that calculated the risk. The business side of him was more analytical. Then there was his emotional side that judged and misjudged. This part of him hid some of his actions from view of my mother who would not have approved.

Like my parents, there were various aspects of me, some hidden from view. Some things stayed locked in little rooms with no windows. They ultimately became blind spots that slowly faded into oblivion, but remained stored within.

What you think no one knows may not be a secret

Hiding things from others requires you to keep them hidden from parts of yourself. The more hidden closets you have the more imbalance there will be. Balancing your intellectual and emotional sides requires inviting them all to the party. The thought is frightening, but when you have a staff meeting with all the inner parts of yourself it helps align your aim directly with your target.

Imagine how much energy could be freed up if you could open the window of enlightenment to all these little rooms.

My quest disclosed a wider angle view revealing hidden perceptions not otherwise apparent. Positioned at the crossroad where my parents' paths crossed two eco-systems intersected. That spot where their paths crossed uncovered blind spots within me. One transformation resulting from my quest was the various parts of me that were forced out of the closet. In business and my personal life a transformation increased my awareness of perceived limitations that had stopped me from mastering my courage to succeed and lead.

One of my most meaningful discoveries was how awareness of blind spots takes away their power to control and sabotage. This opens possibility thinking to new opportunities.

Finding your crossroad uncovers your true potential no matter how deeply it may be hidden. Money and wealth can reap success but a greater contentment is found within. Pursue and find your genuine talents to add more meaning to your achievements. Each step on your journey leads you closer to fulfillment as you consciously dissolve obstacles transforming them into opportunities. Passion and peace allows you to produce better health and more wealth.

Little treasures in this book help you to find the point at the crossroad that leads to success in your business or leadership pursuits. This book is a guide like the map of a golf course to steer you along your journey. It points out the beauty of business that points toward success, but also prepares you for contenders and challenges that threaten to keep you from experiencing your business and leadership potential.

One of the keys to success in business is to find and pursue what you genuinely love. Another is to unlock your passion to pursue it. Imagine the energy locked within you directing your focus to distractions that make you forget those little rooms. Determine who you are and what you love. When you find your passion, there at the crossroad you will find your meaningful pursuit.

As you become aware you find solutions to whatever issues you are facing. Resolving limiting blind spots creates balance and helps you gain clarity in other areas. The newly found, freed up energy gives you more momentum to achieve other more meaningful personal and business goals. Assess your strengths and weaknesses to transform blind spots from threats into opportunities. Resolving blind spots helps you to discover new talents, live healthier, happier and produce more money and wealth.

LINK # 2

SABOTAGE IS A MIRAGE

Running a business seven days a week left me too tired to get on the plane for my planned vacation that Mother's Day weekend. Success in a small business limits vacations to very few. Instead, that morning I went to the golf course where, like my father, I enjoyed hitting golf balls. It is important to release daily stress that comes in running a business. Find an activity that allows your body to get exercise and relaxation.

When my golf ball went out of the well-manicured, unobstructed fairway and into the hazardous rough, I was a little irritated with my performance, but I did not let it bother me. Instead of being frustrated in your business, use your analytical abilities to help you determine what you need to recover. After selecting another club and re-aligning the clubface with the ball and the target, I applied my mental focus to execute a strategy to scoop my ball from the sand. To get out of the bunker, I adjusted my feet shoulder-width apart with my stance slightly open to eleven and one o'clock. Without transferring my weight from my left foot, I turned my shoulders, locked my wrist, and gave a full, relaxed swing to get my ball back on the fairway. I had planned my business to run just as smoothly.

In business it is important to find what rejuvenates your spirit. After hitting golf balls that morning, I went and had a massage. That left me emotionally refreshed, physically invigorated, and mentally charged. I decided to stop by my business on the way home.

Crowds celebrating Mother's Day with their families packed the walkways. Holidays are when people come out to celebrate. On busy days when the business is crowded is when you gain the fastest return on your investment. It is important to have extra staff and plenty of inventory and products to sell.

As I approached, I could see that the neon lights were not on. That's when I first started to feel anxiety.

While drafting my business plan, I had concentrated on a list of key things that were important for business success, including superb staff, good location and great display. It is so hard convincing employees how important the display is for a business. It is the face that customers see. The neon lights are part of that display.

Tough negotiations strategically placed me in an ideal corner on the lower floor. Entrances from two sides and a water view of the adjacent marina allowed customers to approach from their boats, cars or on foot. They could relax along the steamy water's edge and enjoy a delicious cold fruit smoothie. Location is a key factor to business success, whether it is a physical location or online. Customers need to be able to easily access your business. While it would be hard to sell icy drinks online, a website still makes customers aware of your business.

The architectural design of my business allowed the security glass panels that surrounded the business to fold like the pleats of an accordion into the wall. This allowed the business to be completely open to the sidewalk. Security is important but it should not interfere with customers' ability to easily access your business and have a pleasurable experience.

Over-crowding along the sidewalk forced customers closer to the counter where they could enjoy shade from the blistering sun and sample various flavors of delicious healthy thirst-quenching icy drinks made with real fruit. Samples are a good way to advertise for free. Once customers get to know your products and find value they become loyal and keep coming back.

Turning the corner to the entrance, I was shocked to find the security gate to my business closed. Swarms of people walked by. Families celebrating Mother's Day were crowded all around but they could not enter. I saw none of my scheduled staff. Overtaken with anxiety, I pushed open the unlocked gate. My anxiety mounted as my mind raced with thoughts that maybe there had been an accident or my manager had become ill. Adrenaline rushed through my system as I stood in shock. My analytical mind was too cloudy to comprehend what I saw. My highly paid manager was sitting behind the counter in the dark.

"This cannot be real." Every day in business you experience something new, but my intellectual and emotional intelligence combined could not figure this out. Sabotage comes unexpected. This was like a mirage, an optical illusion. That wiped out my early morning vigor.

Without emotional intelligence you judge before knowing the evidence

My God, I thought; its late afternoon, five hours after opening time on one of the busiest holidays of the year. Nothing was set up for the day. The doors remained closed. The cash drawer was not in the cash register. There was no emergency and she was not ill. The horrendous confusion launched me into emotional gridlock. It felt like I was falling through a hole.

When you are in a free fall, it feels like there is no bottom to the center of the earth. **Rapid change can cause you to lose your grip and sharp analytical reasoning goes with it. After the fall is over, the process is not complete. Once you grab a ledge, the worst is over, but that is when you most need to stabilize and engage your intellectual and emotional skills to maintain balance and create a rational solution. Otherwise you will just keep falling.**

Practice emotional fire drills to know your exit in case of an emergency

My appearance shocked her. "Why?" I started to fire off questions. She jumped up and rapidly started setting up while trying to formulate an excuse. But she never gave one.

My intellect combined with my emotions searched the facts, looking for the reasons. I searched my external environment for a logical explanation to help control my emotions. Understanding helps emotions subside.

There was no doubt that she knew the policy to open the business on time. That meant arriving early to set up the business. She also knew that opening late would cost the business a monetary fine.

Pretentious actions suppress your natural abilities

Outwardly, I pretended not to be upset, but deep within every microscopic cell of my body riveted with anger. **Pretentious actions suppress your natural abilities. This causes imbalance that follows you throughout your day. At times it is necessary to fake a tough exterior in order to negotiate your way through a challenging dilemma.**

When I came upon my closed business, it was like I was back in a bunker. I needed something in business like a sand wedge to get me up and out of this slump. Some days in business your alignment is off; you find yourself in the "rough" without a practical technique to apply to a new situation. On the golf course, it is easy to pull a different club out of the bag to get you through each unexpected challenge. The loft of a sand wedge gets you up and out when you find yourself in a hazard.

Immense tension came with my efforts to stop the flaring anger, prevent mental gridlock and do the right thing. Sometimes, in a business emergency it is more important to gain emotional equilibrium than worry about that day's bottom line. Question whether the right thing to do in your situation is the best thing to do. Know that whatever action you take will impact many days to follow. These moments test your best skill as a leader.

My employee had not stolen money from my cash register, but she had kept customers from approaching the counter. Locking customers out had the same effect as stealing in that it prevented money from going into the cash register. This causes revenues to drop drastically and can quickly lead to business failure.

Pilferage, one of the highest cost factors for a business, takes place in many different forms as employees find creative ways to deplete cash from the register or inventory from stock. Pilferage is a blind spot you never see, where business resources are re-allocated or siphoned away from the business. It is difficult to maintain emotional equilibrium when other people's motives are intended to derail the success of your well-laid plans.

Out ragged my emotional right brain equated it to stealing. My analytical left-brain calculated how much money I had lost. This was uncharted territory. In the mists of an emotional storm adrenalin in your body turns on automatically. There is no emergency button to shut it off.

A good staff is a basic fundamental in business. Employees implement your mission through your outlined objectives and are your greatest resource. Therefore, it made sense to hire the best to improve my chances of business success. Flexibly stretching the finances to hire her allowed me to get away. After years and long hours running a small business, what I wanted most was freedom to take a vacation without being called on crisis that dragged me back to the business.

"If you want to grow, you have to spend money to hire the best talent," other successful businessmen advised. I followed the leading edge and hired her as my manager on a salary contract allowing her time to adjust to the business then gain an ownership interest over time. Her contract factored in revenue increases and cost decreases. She was paid more money than any previous employee.

Despite all my efforts to cover all the bases and secure my business, I soon learned that paying a high salary does not mean the staff will produce your desired results. Just because you pay top dollar for an expert does not mean you get the best advice.

Employees are one of your greatest resources, but can also generate your highest costs and cause blind spots that create your greatest risk. Hiring her took my payroll cost over my desired twenty-five percent, but it gave me freedom in return. It took a lot of the pressure off having to run a cash-business fifteen hours a day seven days a week. Some employees, even family partners, do not have the same passion for your business; especially if they have dreams of their own.

I had hired her because she was the most qualified. Looking at her resume, intuitively I knew she was actually overqualified: too intelligent, too educated, too personable, and too articulate for the job. She knew all the right answers. Not wanting to depend on her father's money, she said she needed the job. At the time I needed a good employee and I could not resist hiring the best applicant even though something within me warned that she was not a good fit for my business. Now, I wish I had listened to that inner voice.

The lesson I learned in hiring her taught me the benefits of using intuition and emotional intelligence in business. If I had combined my father's business sense with my mother's intuitive sense and valued both, I would have acted on the warning without learning through experience that her intention was not aligned with the best interest of my business.

I stood at the crossroad wondering who made that decision. Was it me or was it my destiny?

Still trying to understand, I considered all my options. My once sharp intellect was dulled by angry emotions. Mass confusion keeps you searching for nuggets of understanding that help explain the reasons why. Nothing in business or golf prepares you for some mental bunkers. Blurred vision impacts your ability to see clearly. The distraction causes you to feel scattered. This depletes your energy and slows your momentum.

I desperately wanted to fire her and say, "Leave right now." She quickly jumped into action to serve customers rapidly approaching the counter.

Her actions robbed me of a clear analytical thought process to conduct a fair and objective assessment. If I wanted to recover that day's sales, I knew I would need assistance to run the business. Needing time to cool down, I kept silent, smiled and thanked the customers until additional staff arrived. Making a decision in a highly emotional state is not a smart move.

Gaining emotional stability in the emotional right-brain is necessary to allow the analytical left-brain to do the math. *"How much in sales have I lost since I hired her?"*

I had hired her on a contract, agreeing to pay her for two weeks whether she left or stayed. That day's bottom line was already shot, but I could still recover if I acted with speed and emotional intelligence. There was strong inner friction to the thought of working alongside her. Impediments that hinder you also keep you from growing. I had to quickly detach from fuming negative feelings.

Earlier that day on the golf course my ball had gone into the water. The retriever in my golf bag had a swiveling cup at the end allowing me to retrieve balls from the water as long as they were within reach. No matter how much I wanted to recover that ball from the water it was beyond the reach of my retriever. I had to let it go and move on. In the silence on the golf course, I could hear my inner coach nudging me to keep moving. Nature's gentle breeze helps guide you onward with nudging from within.

During my years in business and my many opportunities to judge, observe, and analyze hundreds of employees, this was the one time I misjudged. Your mind throbs when one error trumps all the times you have gotten it right over the years. Your focus and mental clarity are blurred. What gets in the way of rapid action to recover are emotions lurking within.

Although you may be very upset, you do not want to later regret action you have taken. As a small-business owner, essentially, you are the business. "Take deep breaths," I listened to my inner coach just as my mother would often do.

The game of golf gives you a mulligan, which is the opportunity to attempt better performance the second time around. The result, allows you to shake-off a bad shot with a second chance as if the first shot had never been made. Unlike golf, business seldom affords you the luxury of a mulligan to replay a bad shot. Even in golf, a mulligan may handicap you if it becomes a crutch that provides an excuse not to play your best on the first round. If you have little or no skill your second stroke may cause you to appreciate the first one. Without a mulligan it is wise to give your best effort the first time, every time.

Your small business cannot risk the luxury of a mulligan; hoping for better performance the next time. You may not get another chance to re-play your actions in this situation. You may never recover from a shot of bad judgment.

Passion is a plus when used positively

When you are experiencing a negative situation your passion may disastrously drive you downward. Positive thoughts each morning provide serene emotional and mental balance. It is extremely important to apply wisdom to passionate, but negative energies you are feeling. Focusing helps you to control your passion, and quiet the countering sensational noises and strong negative currents going on in your head. This allows you to gain control of the outer situation, which may be totally incongruent with your inner desires and business goals.

Be flexible

Earlier on the golf course, holding my arms too close to my body restricted my golf swing. It allowed little flexibility. Even with the best equipment, my drive would not go far. What was inside of me was getting in the way of my performance, execution, and follow-through.

A vigorous workout on the driving range and nine holes earlier that day left my body relaxed, however, hours later at my business, my body was filled with mental and emotional turbulence. When your body is free from anxiety and mental or physical restriction, it is free to swing faster or execute more accurately. When you are stressed, adrenaline quickly pumps through you.

Too much restriction in your movements or thinking limits your ability to excel. Moving forward towards your goal requires letting go of limitations. Resistance creates a powerful force that pulls you in the opposite direction. Hidden resentments form invisible obstacles that grow into blind spots with the potential to pull you backwards.

In order for a turn around to occur in your performance you have to follow through. Listen to your gentle inner voice coaching, *"Get out of your own way."*

I questioned how I could have better assessed her to determine productivity, performance and more of what was deep within her or at least on her mind. Sometimes you cannot control what other people do but you can control how you physically or mentally respond.

Swallow your pride but not your anger

A sharp surge of emotions can spike your blood pressure, causing physical damage to your body. The result can be catastrophic costing you a stroke in your body. An unfavorable stroke in your golf game is only a temporary setback but for your body it can be fatal. When emotions are provoked to a sufficient intensity and not resolved, a minor situation can easily explode your emotions out of control. Such disturbance can change your mental state and interfere with your equilibrium. Failing to maintain control of your emotions causes a bad situation to worsen, then, you become vulnerable physically. You may later regret something you said. However, holding in your anger can be equally as damaging. Over the long term, losing control may negatively affect your relationships, finances, but most importantly your health.

Control stress with exercise and good nutrition

Although it was early afternoon, the situation had depleted an entire day's energy. What I needed was to rejuvenate, release bottled emotions, and free my flow of energy. A healthy mental game plan for leadership requires a rested and detached mind. When you have a rested mind, you focus better, practice longer, and master your game quicker.

Chaos created by this employee pulled me out of alignment with my purpose to succeed in business knowing that two out of three businesses fail. Striving for success in business over eight years had brought many distracting detours, but none so downright shocking. In business your success is determined by how well you balance, take care of the little things around you, and juggle distractions that clamor for your attention. The busywork created by employee distractions unnecessarily keeps you from your business goal of making money.

Stress weakens your power. Leaders of companies today face outer threats including competitors, threats of a hostile takeover, terrorism, or sabotage. Competition may also come from within your organization. Both inner and outer competitive forces increase red tape to bring stressful elements that dilute your focus. They create doubt and distrust, weaving chaos in your organization. They may also divide your team and cause dis-ease in your entity. The result is a physically weakened ability to execute.

Good nutrition and optimum health habits are important aspects of a leader's game. Whether you are building skills in leadership or working to improve your golf game, practicing relaxation daily is a good habit, too important to be overlooked. The higher you climb up the ladder of business, whether through growth, merger, acquisition, or going public, the more competitive challenges you face, therefore, the more energy and focus you need. The one thing that gives you stamina to stay in the game is good health.

The food you eat if properly digested converts into energy. Improper nutrition may cause a deficiency that leads to an imbalance in your body. When you are under-nourished physically, your body is unprepared. This leads to cravings. It dilutes your energy, redirects your focus away from your primary business goals and hinders you from moving forward.

Plan a quick change for conditions that may be fatal to your bottom line or your health

The situation with this employee made me go deeper within myself. I pondered why I had hired her when I knew clearly that she was not a good fit. The question stayed with me. "Why did I hire her?" That question led to other questions that seemed fairly simple, but like the subtle curves on the putting green earlier that morning, the answers were not readily apparent.

The pieces did not fit, neither analytically nor emotionally. Some answers I needed from her, others only I could provide, including why I hired her knowing she was not right for my business.

She continued working silently as though she had done nothing wrong. No matter what I said she held fast to her self-image and nothing I did could change the picture she maintained of herself. Your reality is not the picture other people see but the picture you hold of yourself. Holding steadfast to your self-image is the primary reason for your success or failure. No one can change it but you. That entire day she never changed the idea of "truth" she held about herself.

As a leader standing on your conviction, there are times when you stand alone. Some things cannot be reasoned with the intellectual mind. Some answers are found only through your inner guidance. I was at this point at the crossroad, forced to humbly allow my inner knowing to guide me. It was then that my business principles began to merge with my spiritual values.

Dealing with this employee-created issue was not in my plans for the day, but like many unexpected urgencies in business it quickly elevated to become a primary issue on my agenda. My ability to focus on the situation was limited by the chaos from the swarm of customers at the counter waiting to be served. I juggled to maintain balance.

Leaders rely on many people to assist in achieving their success. That morning, I relied on only one. Despite all your efforts in business to do it right, sometimes you fail in your attempts to delegate responsibility to a qualified manager. It makes you feel that your business plan is incomplete; failing to have a retreat plan for the unexpected sabotage. What you need is quick action to turn the situation around. Later, you can update your business plan.

No amount of planning can predict every possible outcome in business. That is where inner intelligence becomes important. It helps you to discover things that are not readily apparent. Your intuitive faculties educate you with knowledge about subjects you have never studied. Your inner guide helps you find your way across the water when the bridge runs out.

Be observant of your staff

It became clear that this employee, who I so carefully hand-picked had a different agenda for my business. Her conduct forced me to choose whether to let her go immediately or use her to help me make money. At that moment, she was my only employee. It would have satisfied me immensely to fire her right then, but that would have prevented me from recovering the sales I had already lost that day.

My analytical mind was stuck pondering stealing, sabotage and all kinds of other things. If she was trying to steal money, it would have made more sense for her to open the doors of the business and let in all the customers. That way she could pocket more money. Was she trying to steal? Then why would she leave money on the table. Not taking advantage of the opportunity to pocket the money from customers made her motives seem to be something other than stealing money. Was she under the influence of a foreign substance or had I uncovered a blind spot designed to destroy my business? All these are elements to consider when hiring.

Your business eventually becomes your child. The thought that her actions were designed to destroy it made an emotional part of me harden. Knowing that emotional imbalance can cause you to react very inappropriately made it that much more important to maintain control of my emotions.

Her answers to questions continually did not make sense. She offered no reasons that I could challenge. That left me with my own suspicions. How could I conduct a fair assessment? What measurement could I use? Accepting my limitations my analytical mind was humbled. That's when my intuitive mind became most beneficial.

Both the emotional and analytical parts of me could agree that trust is the cornerstone of successful business ventures. Before you can trust others you have to be able to trust your own decisions. Personally, I wanted to take action that would not have been good for my business. But, what I would lose by doing that could eventually cost me far more.

The need for transparency

Not knowing, what was going on inside her, I suspected that watching her actions would eventually reveal her motives. Her unauthorized actions that morning differed so greatly from the established policies in the company manual. Her actions were not a minor variance but a clear violation that went far beyond the company policies.

Lack of transparency in people keeps relationships in the dark. Manipulation by team mates takes away the safe, trusting environment that allows a team to bond and execute with precision. Secrets introduce deception that is often temporary, until secrets are eventually revealed, however temporary can be a very long time.

Being accountable for the actions of all your employees keeps you mindful that the business needs to keep moving. Instead of taking a firm emotional stand, sometimes it is more important to flexibly follow your conviction to fulfill the business mission. Getting through my situation required compressing negative energy to focus all attention on my most important and primary business goal of making money.

Machines are not motivated by greed or prejudice

Working next to her brought up thoughts of wanting to replace her with a machine. Machines do not sabotage; they simply function. Properly designed machines have one advantage because they carry no emotional baggage. For this reason they can be more productive. In my heat of passion, it was difficult to set aside emotions and objectively ponder the downside of machines. While technology increases speed, the human factor offers a smile, something that technology cannot give. I calculated costs, benefits and motives. People's ability to distort accurate information, manipulate the bottom line, and conspire out of greed, hatred, jealousy or other emotions impact the bottom line. These were not issues I had considered when I started my business, but were new realities I had to face.

Clarity helps you recover from sabotage

Small business owners face the same business challenges as leaders in major corporations, only on a smaller scale. Sabotage stops your forward momentum and emotionally takes you backwards. These issues keep business leaders from being present. Anticipate challenges and command your attention to the next step on your roadmap. As you encounter roadblocks, keep a clear vision of your contingency plan in the forefront of your mind.

Success requires turning the situation around to continue moving forwards. It is important after every disappointment to take time to reflect and gain clarity. Rather than allowing mishaps to derail you, use them as learning lessons to clear the path for your future performance. Go back to find the point where the problem first appeared. Analyze how and why the malfunctions happened. Determine what went wrong. Apply what you learn to rapidly adapt your future performance. Measure results testing different hypothetical's, but keep your momentum moving forward.

Review your clearly defined business goals and strategic plans regularly. Analyze more than one way of getting there. Sabotage is like a sand trap on the golf course. To recover take aim then with a full swing execute your game plan and blast your way out of that bunker.

When people withhold information it indicates ulterior motives and requires use of your inner vision

More deep breaths kept me calm. At least I appeared that way. "Why?" Again I waited for an explanation but none came.

When I started in business I had clarity of focus and a vision. I had never experienced this kind of sabotage. Now behind the counter, looking through the mental fog, my vision was blurred making it hard to see. I was forced to start observing not only with my eyes but also with my inner vision. This lesson came from my mother.

Physical activities on the golf course and positive mental thoughts had kept me grounded in the past. Now, my emotions were wildly floating in and out of rage, requiring continual positive mental conversations with whatever part of me that would listen.

No matter what I was experiencing behind the counter, good customer service required that I give customers my best. I had to take deep breaths and talk to myself. It is not easy to manage your emotions when you are down in the gutter. It was difficult to force a smile right then, even for customers who deserved it. The longer I held a smile the more natural it felt as customers quickly approached the counter. They knew nothing about my dilemma. I had always given my best and they simply wanted the same consistent service that kept them coming back.

Blind spots in business

An objective in golf is to keep the ball moving forward. Each stroke in golf advances you closer to the flag. Taking action in business also keeps the flow of momentum moving towards your target. Blind spots obstruct your view of the target. On the golf course it may be a tree. In business it may be motives of other people. Blind spots have the potential to hinder you as long as they remain hidden in the dark. They lurk at unexpected moments and sabotage your efforts to move forward. Bringing them to light helps them to disappear. Ego, resignation and pride within you, your staff or competitors can also form blind spots that get in the way of solutions when they prevent new methods from being applied to remedy a situation. This only causes the issue to grow more out of hand.

Insight is a form of enlightenment that liberates you from the dark. Beyond the blind spots, you discover your inner essence. Understanding helps you trust and a strong character helps you follow your inner road signs.

Use emotional intelligence to leverage leadership

Research overwhelmingly shows that up to ninety percent of one's performance effectiveness is due to emotional savvy rather than technological knowledge. Unlike Intellectual intelligence (IQ), which is considered to be set from childhood on, emotional intelligence (EQ) can be developed with age and maturity. IQ is a measure of one's cognitive abilities. It measures spatial and mathematical reasoning, verbal comprehension, information and memory.

Emotional Intelligence involves components of emotional self-awareness, including managing one's own emotions, using emotions to maximize intellectual processes, developing empathy, using the art of social relationships and managing emotions in others. Emotional intelligence comes into play in various business settings, including, selling to customers, hiring employees and negotiating in business deals.

Increasing your emotional intelligence also enhances your relationships in other areas. Connecting with the buying emotions of your customers helps you to close the sale faster. These emotions include: greed that wants to keep up with the Jones; fear that looks for things that are guaranteed or proven; flattery that wants to be complimented; guilt that needs to know it's ok; exclusivity that constantly looks for new, innovative products; anger that seeks justice; redemption that needs solutions; ego-oriented dominance; fear of being taken advantage of; or a primary fear of social rejection. This gives your relationship stability. The need for stability accounts for much of the U. S. population, especially in today's time of uncertainty.

Regulators are critical thinkers, fearful and low risk takers. They seek accountability, look for quality control, and are likely to be in fields of engineering, banking and science. You have to motivate them to buy, use data and facts, examine the pros and cons from all sides, and give proven solutions. They do not respond well to hard sells. Their greatest fear is criticism.

Balance is an essential ingredient in the recipe for success

One of the earliest experiences of balance is learning to ride a bike. Obstacles are the hurdles, like the cracks in the side-walk for a child learning to ride a bike. They create anxiety that prevents a smooth ride. Before you learn to balance your skill, you experience anxiety. This comes from doubt in a child's ability to ride. Initially, without support the ride is jittery. They sway from side to side. Slowly they learn to apply different techniques such as shifting their weight from side to side, turning the handle bars, or putting down their feet, to keep from falling. Children experience and learn how to negotiate quick turns to avoid bumps.

Eventually, they fall. The fall helps them to resolve uncertainty by gauging the distance from the ground and feeling the pain of falling. This is an essential part of the development of self-confidence. Support helps them recover from the fall, get up and try again. After a little coaxing they experience the actual ride without the training wheels. As skills develop they gain more flexibility and trust in their own ability. Support does not keep them from falling it only cushions the fall. If you stop or prevent their fall you impede their growth. Continuing to ride is a necessary process that reduces their risk and fear of falling.

People do not like failing but continuing the process of riding and falling helps to develop key components for self-confidence. Continued support from family and friends lessens anxiety and builds trust that develops into positive self-talk, enjoyment and passion. Parents that try to keep their children from experiencing a fall do not help them develop self-confidence because the process is incomplete.

Anxiety exists when there is uncertainty. Without completing the experience of the actual ride, the concept of riding is more like a vague theory. Lurking within you anxiety remains unresolved. Uncertainty about your performance or the fear of falling leaves other doubts unresolved, "Can I do it?" or "Will I fall?" Later in life the word, "fall" turns into the word, "fail". "Will I fail?" It becomes a question that constantly lingers in your head. You focus more on failing than succeeding.

A child's concerns about falling continue to loom. "Will it hurt?" Pain may be internal or external depending on your experience. When the emotions of fear and pleasure exist at the same time, it is said that fear will always control. Children are resilient and quickly recover from physical pain. The more lasting pain for a child may be an emotional scare or the pain that comes from not having support to pick them up when they fall.

As children grow into adults the subtle fears turn into awkward feelings. It is hard to describe how awkward feels. For some it is subtle for others it causes great anxiety. The greater the anxiety the more likely you are to avoid or take action to reduce the pain. Disregarding subtle pains keep them dormant within you. Years later they develop blind spots to hinder your success.

EQ provides detours to get around obstacles

Some obstacles between you and your goal are generated by internal factors. It is easier to see road blocks that others throw into your path but not so easy to see when you are the road block. This is where emotional intelligence is most useful. When you can look and see obstacles ahead you are forewarned to be prepared by tightening your grip. Emotional intelligence lights your path to help you understand yourself better. This inner development then gives you a better understanding of your team, despite all their unique differences.

Destruction indicates a lack of emotional intelligence. Some leaders fail to understand how needlessly depleting company resources affects their job security. It costs the company more. When expenditures continue to exceed revenues, it leads to financial imbalance. Leaders who do not see that the business income is what generates their household income are shortsighted. Maintaining well balanced personal finances is impossible if the business that generates your personal income goes under. Indications of lack of emotional intelligence include, distorting, shifting or deleting data, blowing things out of proportion, twisting and stretching the truth. Emotional Intelligence not only helps in hiring employees, but also makes better employees.

The negative energy of destruction lingers long after the damage is restored. Destruction hurts innocent bystanders. To decrease the likely impact of future damage, anticipate these risks and prepare a plan to get through.

Emotional intelligence respects the intelligence of your customers. Manipulation sells to their ignorance. Emotional intelligence helps to develop the habit of tackling subtle fears, underlying doubts and self-imposed limitations that hold leaders back from realizing their ultimate potential that leads to enjoyment and greater success.

Emotional intelligence helps you to become a better judge of character. It balances you like a pendulum. A pendulum is a weight that hangs from a rod, balanced in its resting position. It freely swings suspended from an anchor, it oscillates swinging back and forth equal distance in opposite directions. The pendulum is a perfectly timed gadget. Throwing a pendulum in one direction causes it to come swinging back in the opposite direction, equal distance from its center.

The pendulum is an example of balance, but it also demonstrates physical or emotional lack or excess, in the body's perfectly timed mechanical pendulum causing it to swing towards physical or emotional cravings when there is lack or the opposite extreme of excess. Being under-nourished physically or emotionally in one area causes an imbalance that urges you to take in excesses in another area. This can easily result in overindulging in food or other things.

Just like a pendulum that swings equally from side to side, if there is imbalance in your belief system your internal pendulum swings equally to the other side and urges behavior that displays a revolution in the opposite extreme. This is where you began to lose control. This is not good for your business. The health of a business like physical health needs balance and flexibility. Rigidity in the muscles causes contractions. Similarly, rigidity in the business causes either financial bulging or recession. Flexibility helps you take a necessary check and balance in times when it may be needed.

Keeping your resources balanced is as important as balancing your weight on a bike to keep from falling. Having the best equipment in golf is just a start, but it's not enough to win the game. Having a large amount of resources in business does not guarantee success either.

Developing emotional balance helps you succeed using both your emotional and your intellectual mental computer. Balance gives you a stable footing and develops into confidence. It is one lesson that cannot be taught, it must be experienced.

Handling a turnaround

Without some catastrophe or sabotage, thriving successful businesses that stay ahead of the trends may never face a turnaround. A catastrophe happens quickly. Sabotage, on the other hand may drain the books slowly for years before being uncovered. When you discover that action is needed, stop and examine your resources, then make a change in the direction of your mission.

The objective of a turnaround in business is to gain stability and produce improvement in performance. What gets turned around is a trend from declining results to improving results, from loses to profits. These are the measurable results of a turnaround that indicate success.

A turnaround is needed where a division of a company or the total organization is on a downward trend, consistently performing below average, compared to prior figures or its industry or sector.

When your child gets failing grades on a report card, you take immediate action to remedy the situation by getting a tutor for additional help. The tutor you get will depend on the exact area where help is needed. The same should apply when a business is bleeding and a turnaround is necessary. It is not a situation to allocate blame or where pride prevents one from taking action. The more intelligent thing to do is acknowledge that a bleeding wound needs attention to stop the bleeding. Quick action gives the business an opportunity to apply special remedies to turn the situation around.

Efforts in a turnaround are designed to raise performance and revenue. Your options are to shun or embrace a turnaround. If you remain in an unproductive, resigned state with a blind spot blocking your mental view, it is hard to see that you need help. In the alternative if you embrace it, you can become an opportunity-oriented, action seeking visionary whose major concern is the overall interest of getting the business stable and healthy again.

Accurately assess the business and its leaders

A business plan allows you to keep score of where you started, where you are and where you are going. The next step is to search for imbalances that lead to blind spots. It takes an objective critical eye to get an accurate assessment. A proper assessment feeds your mind questions that lead to other questions and ultimately unlock and open awareness.

Look in cost of goods sold to see if there is too much inventory or not enough. Running out of inventory between orders is a sign of not enough or inventory is walking out the door. See if payroll is out of alignment, too many on staff to serve a few customers or not enough staff, causing the business to lose customers who do not want to wait in line. Analyze excessive expenses, bulging assets, low sales or not enough cash on hand. Are there supply issues involving inability to get deliveries or product, unhealthy competition, or other issues eroding demand or market share?

Accurate sales and expenses reported in the financials indicate where leaks may be taking place to drain the bottom line. Closer internal examinations tell the whole story. Further assessments confirm the exact problem and its location. The degree and type of action depends upon the extent of the damage. Mending the results of either catastrophe or sabotage requires fast and possibly undesirable action to quickly regain stability. The goal is to return the business running smoothly and profitably in the black as quickly as possible with the least amount of resources.

Without an accurate measurement it is hard to get a true assessment. Accurate financials give you the best gauge. In the situation with my business, it would have been hard for me to get a true understanding why my sales had dropped on that Mother's Day if I had not unexpectedly stopped by my business that morning and seen the financial drain or sabotage occurring. Having secret shoppers visit your business can make this same discovery.

Looking at my decision to go into business and to hire an employee with an unassuming nature, even though she was wrong for my business, left me wondering, "Who made that decision?" Some of my business decisions were decisions that my parents would have made, but they were nowhere around at the time. Looking deeper into other major decisions I began to see just how each decision merged right near the point where my father's thinking crossed my mother's thinking.

Strangely, it appeared I had found some ingredients in the recipe for my assignment. Somewhere deep within me my parents still existed. Bound to the same perceptions as my parents had been, like a pet chained to a tree on a six-foot chain? If nothing changes within me, I could only expect to go as far as their reasoning allowed me.

Perceptions of your parents, things you do not know are controlling decisions that you make. Most people never live up to their full potential. That trait continues unless you use time to change the future's outcome. Time is the one resource that allows you to achieve all your dreams. Don't take it for granted.

Suddenly I realize I need to hurry up, rigorously and genuinely embrace the future with my own game plan to turn this thing around. Time is quickly ticking.

Know when to fold

I finally find a balanced approach that quiets both my analytical left brain and my emotional right brain. What I had to fold and give up were the negative emotions I held. Both business and golf require constant decision making, monitoring, and adjustments to each stroke of execution. Success in business requires those decisions to be quick

My decision to let the matter go reduces my anxiety and allows me to focus and move forward. I consider a backup strategy for events that could alter that plan. Staying emotionally upset makes it hard to remain true to my business purpose and myself. While I analyze the situation at the front counter I can hear the cash register ringing. That makes it easier to give up my anger against her.

Seeing happy customers helps pull me back to center. Making money and satisfying my customers were more important than assuaging my anger. That helps me to stay in alignment with my business goal of making money. Smiling, even if forced, changes your physiology and creates a change in the way you feel. When you smile at others who know nothing about your condition, they give back smiles.

In business and in golf, the benefits of some shots pay off in the short range; other shots pay off in the far and distant future. Blind spots keep you from seeing your target. Lack of proper set-up and interference with your focus take you out of alignment when you execute. I stood on the shrubbery-lined landscape of business right at the point of execution. Success requires a clear view ahead.

LINK # 3

ASSESSMENTS UNCOVER BLIND SPOTS

Finding your crossroad starts with a thorough assessment of the past and your idea of it. A deep inner analysis exposes you to who you really are. This is good practice for what you will need in business, including gathering and processing information, implementing choices, and making decisions.

Plan your business day in tiny increments down to the smallest detail. Failing to plan, is planning to fail, because when you fail to define your goals, expectations set by others become your target. A goal that is not yours has no passion. If your goal is not within you it keeps you looking outward. Dedication to a continuous process requires discipline, which works best with passion.

Assessing your past helps reveal whether you have the capacity to stay committed to what will be a continuous process. Examining the past for what worked and what did not work helps to unveil potential blind spots or indicate what you may encounter in the future.

Diligently study yourself be willing to look inside

Performance is influenced to a large degree by self-image. Self-image is the sum total of all beliefs you hold about yourself. Companies have self-images also. How you see yourself, as a business person is how you function. To act otherwise creates psychological inconsistency and leads to imbalance. A company becomes a mirror image reflecting the people in it. High personal self-esteem spreads and results in high productivity in the business. The contrary also holds true.

Humbly assess your own strengths and flaws to gain clarity in your vision and better understand the strengths and weaknesses of others. To lose a hole in golf does not hurt your pocketbook but in business, especially small business, to execute a game plan with inaccurate data or to recover from sabotage could incur a serious financial blow.

Searching is the process that generates answers. It helps you to accelerate forward. There is something about your human will power; it can take away all fear and doubt when you decide what you will do. Replace worry and uncertainty with accurate assessments and courage to play your best shot. Create a habit of challenging and tackling "head on" subtle fears, everyday doubts and self-imposed limitations that hold you back from realizing your maximum potential and your highest level of enjoyment and success.

A thorough analysis considers various aspects of your personal, family, financial, social, and spiritual life. Look through various lenses for historical, futuristic, political, and economic perspectives. During the analytical process, the only thing you should want to know is, will it lead to improved performance. Expect that growth may initially shake up your current stability and order. It is called change; the necessary change that keeps you from failing.

Consider that with regard to failure, the best solution to get over the fear of failing may be to actually fail. It helps you realize, like falling off a bike, you simply pick yourself up and continue riding. Anticipate what you could salvage. Shake-up may be useful to jolt you out of limiting projections from the past that keep your dreams behind you. The desire to succeed begins to propel you forward again. Once you experience growth, it is hard to go back.

During the examination process, evaluate and understand the consequences of failure. Dissolve fears of failure so success rather than failure becomes your motivator. Expect criticism. Some obstacles are simply psychological distortion. Pull back the covers of blind spots that impede efforts. Determine what it takes to implement your vision or, if necessary, how to modify your performance to make success happen.

Be complete but creative in your assessment. The greater obstacles you overcome in your mind, the more flexible you are to mentally stretch into that new reality. Make a list of what-if questions going out as far as you can. Have courage to push the limits of experimentation. Assessments help you find the optimum balance for your spiritual, mental, emotional, physical, and financial well-being. With dedication and commitment to go within, you learn to diagnose your own problems where you find lasting solutions.

To help find your meaningful purpose ask yourself: What gifts have I been given? What beauty have I created in my life? Other than myself, what or who else can I find to love? Take no shortcuts here because business is a jealous mistress and will have a profound impact on your personal relationships.

A thorough personal assessment helps you refine your attitudes about success and prosperity, and to align them with your boundaries of integrity. In business you will be tested. Study your limits and where you give up when faced with insurmountable odds. The more accurate your projections the better you are able to shape the destiny of your business. As your business matures you will be constantly applying applications to make it better? A developmental review includes an analysis of your personal growth as well as the growth of the business.

Study diligently how you can unlock more of your potential to raise your self-esteem. Practice doing it consciously and controllably through positive self-talk and watch good things begin to happen for you. Accurately examine life, work, family, then consider the relationship between them. Deep inquiry helps you to gain clarity of your boundaries. Assess deeper to make your vision more vivid, enticing and inspiring. Answers come through various forms, including inspiration as you align with your evolutionary path. The more you assess both your personal and business you will find what ignites your passion.

Each time you make a decision you encounter a series of options. Each choice leads to a different path. Within each choice is opportunity. When you make a decision know the consequences and the reasons to justify it. Don't be left regretting, asking, "What made me make that choice? I didn't see that coming. My life could have been different."

Know the options for your choices. Be clear when you say, "This is what I recommend. This is why I recommend it." Know your premise, analysis, and conclusion. There are so many things around you that you do not know, many things you miss. When you encounter blind spots, slow down and adjust your mirror.

Assess people including your staff and customers

Your assessment gives you a road map especially when scheduling employees to work together. You gain answers to questions like are they introverted or extroverted, verbal or non-verbal? Do they enjoy teamwork? Are they task or people oriented? Do they think logically, seeking data when they lack understanding or when there is a need to know? Do they utilize caution, avoid or take risk; prefer to do things themselves or do they prefer to delegate? Are they responsible in delegating? Do they gravitate toward quality control? Do they want others to notice them? Do they avoid or gravitate towards conflict? Do they have a need to be in charge or to be right? Do they care more about stability or the opportunity to take extreme risks? Do they accommodate others?

Assess the leadership style of your team to learn how and what motivates them. Prepare for excitement in your business. You will meet many new people. Question your customers to determine how satisfied they are and what about your product is more appealing today than yesterday. Customers give the best insight into how your products solve their problems. Next to your customers, your suppliers offer a ton of information.

Study your upper management, and your ground floor staff. Monitor your percentage of payroll costs. If it is too high, maybe your staff is not returning the investment it is costing you to keep them employed.

Are you too removed from the ground floor? If so, you are probably just as removed from your customers. In this case, it is likely that you are not targeting your specific market niche; instead you may be spaying marketing dollars across the general public.

The more you know about your customer, the better you are able to satisfy them. By knowing their needs and problems, you are able to tailor your products and marketing to meet those needs.

Do you know the cultural similarities of people in similar age groups? What distinguishes the generations; "X", "Y" and "Baby-Boomers" other than their ages? What are their learning styles? Do you know what your customers are saying, how they view your business? How can you expect customers to be loyal if you don't really know who they are?

Baby Boomers represent a large population born in the United States between approximately 1943 and 1964. Associated more with affluence and privilege, in general they are wealthier, more active, and physically fit than generations before them. They have become accustomed to this lifestyle; creating expectations that the world will improve. They tended to be less traditional, less formal, and less loyal, representing dramatic social change. Before the economic crisis they controlled over 80 percent of personal financial assets and more than half of all consumer spending. The subprime mortgage and financial crisis especially hit the baby boomers who are said to have lost 60 percent value in investments because of the economic crisis. As a result, 42 percent have been forced to delay retirement. Baby boomers are associated with civil rights, feminist causes, gay rights, handicapped rights, and right to privacy. Focusing on personal issues like dwindling finances as a result of the financial crisis, caused attention to be directed away from social issues that began to unravel and disintegrate. Whatever may be argued in favor of or against baby boomers, the one fact is that their sheer force of numbers creates a norm.

The Generation X population, born between 1965 and 1982, came after the baby boomer generation. They were highly educated and most associated with technology, the savings and loan crisis, and the 1990's boom which contributed to their wealth. Claims for this generation, also known as the "Me" generation range from balanced, happy and family oriented at one extreme to materialistic, slackers, and disenfranchised at the other end.

The Generation X, would give you 42 million customers. However, in order to satisfy them you must know what they need. They are not inspired or attracted by promise of a rosy future. They want immediate satisfaction. The previous generation of

Baby Boomers was successful in their time but failed to readjust to a new generation who are only pacified getting the reward now. Disappointed Baby Boomers who took out second mortgages on their homes to send their Generation X children off to get a college education did not know that their strategy was obsolete. The "rosie future" only appealed to their Baby Boomer Generation. The "Generation X" children did not want to wait to finish college. They set out on their own, leaving their Baby Boomer parents with outstanding balances on their mortgages used to finance student loans. Parents did not think their own children would leave them stranded. However, like business owners who failed to do their marketing research or who discounted the power of trends, suffered financially with little return on their investments.

The Generation Y or Millennial Generation is a class unique unto itself, with a range of birthdates generally between 1978 and 2000, but have been found as early as 1976 and as late as 2004. They are associated with the enlightened 2000 coming-of-age, and most influenced by digital technologies. They send up to 50 text per day. They are skeptical of advertising and institutions, including the institution of marriage. Only 20 percent of them are married as opposed to 42 percent of baby boomers. Millennials have a tolerance and diversity for religious, racial, gender, and sexual orientation differences. They make up 20 percent of the same sex marriages. They are the hardest hit by the economic crisis; suffering from high unemployment and living with their parents longer. They are concerned about economic equality, social justice, and making a difference. Less interested in commitment to a political institution, Millennials have high faith in political independents. They are sometime s known as the Trophy Generation reflecting the trend in competitive sports, where mere participation is frequently enough for a reward. Confidence and tolerance are their attributes; assertively seeking feedback makes communication more important for them. With greater expectations, they switch jobs more frequently. Social change has been accelerated by smart phones, social media and mobile computing. Said to make up 30 percent of the U.S. population, targeting this group would give you 80 million, racially diverse, economically stressed, politically liberal consumers who want to run their own businesses. Targeting the Millennial or Y Generation is most effective through graphical user interface or visual languages. They spend now rather than saving for tater. What gave meaning to earlier generations offer little to Millennials. For them the world has definitely become smaller, with greater variety of diversity. It would take a member of the Millennial generation to resolve the Middle East crisis.

Understand the identity and values of your customers and employees. This is equally important as understanding yourself and other aspects and processes of your business.

Issues to monitor in business

In mergers and acquisitions a comprehensive due diligence process is conducted. An organization has a fiduciary responsibility to obtain an accurate portrait of the prospective organization through a process that reviews public and private documents in areas of primary focus for the organization, including history, mission statement, organizational values, vision statement, integrity program, environmental initiatives, policies and practices, conflict of interest disclosure policy and processes, relationships with competitors, services accepted from outside entities, memberships on outside entity's board, the nature of business transactions entered into for the sale, exchange or lease of property, lending money or extension of credit, furnishing of goods, services, equipment or facilities leases, payment or reimbursement of any kind, other family members currently employed, or employees being compensated by competitors, participation in devices or processes giving entitlement to royalty payments, including patents, design, rights, trademarks, copyrights; holding associated ownership interest, engaging in any other personal activity or relationship where decisions may be influenced, any position allowing personal gain, referrals to an outside supplier, potential for gain other than salary, including any compensation or investment interest. Finally, a merger would examine where the signor of the due diligence certifies compliance and agrees to report should any other conflicts arise.

Since a small business is not held to these same standards of inquiry as a merged organization, the assessment need not replicate the complicated processes of a large business. However, the same thorough assessment could benefit frugality and productivity to ensure the survival of the small business and help it to grow into a large business.

Assess yourself and your business venture in the same manner as a merger due diligence. When your business mission statement reflects your inner values, you are more likely to accomplish and be satisfied with the final result. Address all aspects concerning the business venture you are considering. After considering all the obstacles, then prepare to confront them. That is when you encounter yourself. Constantly prepare for new opportunities. Expectancy helps you to go through that door when it opens.

Clarifying your values increases personal awareness and strengthens your foundation. As you get to know yourself it reinforces your self-trust. Personal growth leads to greater self-expression. You will find your cross road when you are willing to intrude into the unfamiliar areas of yourself.

Questions to consider in a business assessment

An intense assessment of yourself, further assess and examine your business structures, processes, projects, and plans for implementing your objectives. Do you really understand the numbers reflected in your financial statements? Can you trust the source of your information? How well have you analyzed the risk factors and rewards, timetables and benchmarks for your business?

Look deeper into your decision to go into business, examine your passions and how authentically you treasure each aspect of your business goals. Question, anticipate, and imagine your success in pursuing this venture, but don't ignore the possibility that you may still face sabotage or other challenges.

When you first start a business, you start with your idea of who you are. It takes time for the old image you have of yourself to change to reflect the new person pursuing a new dream. In business you learn how difficult it is to change human behavior, that of others and yourself. Resistance prevents change in a new direction. Through repetition in executing your daily business activities the process grows into a learned habit. Eventually, the image you have of yourself changes. It may take more time for others around you who knew the old you to recognize or acknowledge the new you.

Consciously take the plunge

Despite the weight of analytical evidence recommending that I stay put, something inside said go. My decision to leave a secure position for the uncertainty of a new business start-up turned out to be a good one. How could I arrive at that decision when the analytical evidence alone screamed, "No?"

Combined with your logical mind, your emotional mind gauges the probabilities or certainties of your decisions such as leaving a secure position, funding or support to go into business. My decision to go into business gave a surprising sense of freedom. Working longer hours, nearly twice as hard gave a greater sense of accomplishment than being an employee because the success or failure of the business was riding on my efforts. The business returned a financial reward greater than I ever expected. This confirmed my inner knowing and calculated better than all the analytical evidence, which recommended that I stay put.

Going into business is like jumping off a cliff. No one can tell you when to jump. That is something only you know. When you jump without solid inner confirmation, is when you look back with regret. Before you commit to go into business understand the business processes thoroughly, but more importantly know your own internal makeup. Know the real reason why you are doing it. Is it for the money, the title, to pacify or support a family member or to fulfill a meaningful purpose?

In a quiet corner where you can hear yourself think, diligently assess your desire. Carefully balance it with the required investment of time and money and the commitment necessary to keep it going. Never stop studying to see what new insights you can learn about yourself. Anticipate new challenges, including the naysayers you can expect to encounter each day.

Lack of clarity dims your inner light and slows you down. As you gain clarity, signals from within indicate when it is time to proceed. Follow those inner lights, especially when the way is dark, but anticipate a cliff ahead. Inner yellow lights are indications to slow down, apply caution, especially when the business revenues are sliding downward. Like arrows on the golf course pointing you in the right direction to the next tee, inner green lights indicate when it's safe to go full speed ahead with that dream you hold in your heart. As you gain courage, accelerate your efforts.

Finally, decide on a course of action. With an accurate assessment decisions are made easy. If assessed properly your business will be a meaningful pursuit.

Your internal computer crunches a thorough analysis then processes the information. This is the same internal computer that intimately knows each tap of your heart beat. It knows the point where your father's path crosses your mother's path. It leads you to the edge, but then, you have to jump in order to confirm your leadership path.

When you open the lid to look inside yourself, it is unpredictable whether you will find more challenges or more gifts. Inside of Pandora's Box she found many human ills but at the bottom there was hope. Sometimes growth is completely terrifying, yet, there is also the possibility that it opens up a future of new beginnings. Be ready when you ask, you may get what you are asking sooner than you realize.

Some people complain about working too hard at their job, so they leave and go into business. Changing status from employee to business owner is the biggest promotion you will ever receive. It puts you at the top of the hierarchy. Everyone else now punches a clock. The position of CEO makes you responsible for all of your team's actions. In a small business the title CEO really means supervisor, manager and chief janitor over everyone and everything. All the work and all the decisions now rest with you to perform or delegate.

Remember all the things you complained about as an employee, now, as CEO you have the power to resolve them. With the stroke of a pen you can change them to your liking. You quickly learn that it is not so simple. If you did not want to work hard as an employee, nothing will change; you will not like working hard in your business.

As an employee, it is easy to wake up and call-in to take sick leave or time off work. You are paid to take a vacation. That changes when you become CEO of your own business. Things that previously did not matter now do. Whether or not you turned off the lights when you walked out the door as an employee, did not matter but now it does. It increases your costs. Included with the title CEO are all the complaints, plus all the bills.

As an employee you generally have one boss. In business you have many. Sandwiched between your employees and your customers, not to mention your suppliers, can be suffocating. Customers become your real boss because satisfying them controls whether you survive and how long you remain in business. As long as you keep them happy customers will keep coming back. Happy means that your prices must be right for the products you offer. It means that the quality of the products must be satisfactory. More importantly, it means that some deeper need within your customer is being met. This keeps them loyal.

In business, you walk a fine line between keeping your customers and your employees happy. Imagine that the kind of personality you had as an employee is the kind of staff you will attract. Some employees care about their jobs, others simply work for the money. Still others are there to sabotage the business.

It is your job as CEO to know the kind of character you hire because you are ultimately responsible for all their actions. After considerable training to enhance their skills, you sometimes learn that an employee has decided to leave just when you have no replacement. This puts you in a delicate position. A more threatening position is when manipulation by an employee basically holds you hostage in your business.

Finding the crossroad of your father and your mother's path requires going back in time and may even take you through an unpleasant past. Expect the path to be sprinkled with challenges. If your quest is to pursue a business venture, first, determine whether it is the right path and second, measure your passion and commitment, because you will be tested. Monitor regularly and confirm often that you are still on the right road.

If you wake up the morning after and discover you have entered into a bad partnership, the quicker you realize it will never get any better, the quicker you can detach and force a turnaround. If you are headed in the wrong direction, no amount of commitment or hard work will get you where you want to go. In fact, your journey will be harder because you must first detach emotionally from the wrong path, then shift to the right road.

There are times in business when you experience a personal transformation. At other times your business will be turned around. Part of the fulfillment that comes from pursuing a worthwhile challenge is admiring how you overcame insurmountable obstacles that could have easily turned you around, or turned your business upside down. Ultimately, those same challenges built the character of a leader and gave your business the foundation to survive.

The beginning of the journey, getting out of the gate and the end of the journey, evolving are the two hardest parts of your pursuit. In between are the challenges riddled with obstacles that force you to dig deeper to stay committed to the journey. Obstacles unsteady your balance, testing your ability to conquer your own doubt. Staying focused on your vision helps you to find answers no matter what obstacles may appear. Embrace the peaks as well as the valleys. Never give up in the middle. Keep going the entire distance. Use introspection, contemplation, and transformation to conquer the blind spots that are lurking.

A personal or business assessment helps you to get to the core of you. You have to strip away all the unnecessary baggage in the business and in yourself. Finding your purpose requires you to get beyond all the stuff that has clogged your emotional arteries and resulted in false beliefs about who you are. Digging deeper allows you to find your truth and determine what it takes for success. Then take charge to pursue your purpose with passion and drive.

The purpose of that initial thorough analytical assessment was to help uncover blind spots that limit your personal flexibility to perform or that hinder your business production. Then you develop emotional intelligence to complete your intended mission, know when to let go, or how to detach and move on.

After a thorough assessment, the next step of crafting your vision is to test your formula. Shape it through planning, mold it through commitment. When you jump off a cliff, it's exhilarating but fearful. You learn to take nothing for granted.

LINK # 4

KEY INGREDIENTS FOR LEADERSHIP SUCCESS

E arlier that day, wanting better results on the golf course I challenged myself at each hole. There was always something to improve, but there was also progress to celebrate.

Know your leadership style

The higher your leadership role the greater your vision becomes. Fundamental traits of a successful leader include a balanced personal character, willingness to learn, high self-esteem, strong personal convictions, being team-oriented, a risk taker, motivator and a visionary. Other traits for success in business include: the ability to lead with a velvet hammer, desire and courage to transform, plus positive attitude and high energy. Powerful leadership attributes also include effective listening skills, questioning techniques and the ability to influence people.

Leaders are rewarded for their talent to select managers who execute with excellence, create an environment of team spirit that inspires individuals and the team to pursue goals and consistently achieve results substantially greater than they would on their own.

Personal styles that create a win-win atmosphere include, being persuasive, a possibilities creator and a good communicator. It helps a leader to enjoy people, adhere to high standards, and laugh easily.

Delegate and accept responsibility

To fearlessly lead through tough times you have to accept enormous amounts of responsibility. First and foremost be responsible for yourself. Some people do not like accepting responsibility; understand this when you delegate. Delegating requires you to trust another person. The result is that it reduces your burdens and frees up time for more important planning. Successful leaders learn to trust responsibly.

Develop a strong sense of personal responsibility for your team so that each understands that the one person you are accountable for is you. Responsibility is pro-active.

Develop a decision making process. After your assessment choose to decide then choose to act wisely. There may be times of fear, but have fear because you choose it. At times when you do not choose fear, then choose courage. Be wise in your choosing.

Accepting accountability lightens the weight of self-imposed resistance. This allows clarity to improve your vision and accelerate your growth. A strong sense of identity and responsibility helps you get through the tough times and when you get lost in clouds of confusion.

Know if you are a visionary or an implementer

Vision gives you a sense of direction and sets you on a clear path towards your goal. Success in business is limited to your inner and outer vision. You cannot accomplish any more than a goal you can see. Blind spots in business, like in golf, block your view.

Fortunately, the golf course is littered with road signs that help you find detours around the obstacles. However, blind spots in business are less apparent with little, if any, warning.

Like the fourteen clubs in your golf bag with different angles, leaders have different angles and styles. Some leaders are visionaries others are implementers. Visionaries have a greater vision to see the big picture, while implementers manage people and details necessary to carry out the vision. Successful visionaries know their strengths and also know their weaknesses. They move out of the way for their vision to be executed.

Successful execution requires knowing what angle is right for a particular situation. Your performance as a leader improves with a flexible approach that lets you move out of the way when it helps you win the game.

As you become more experienced in assessing people you will know what leadership styles work best and which ones to avoid. These may include, arrogant, self-absorbed, aggressive, inflexible to redirection, and those who are violators of standards or impractical and not present.

True visionaries are not good implementers

In the strategic planning process the CEO is the visionary. The CEO sits high and dreams about things no one else can see. Others on the team execute the minute details, tactics and action steps. Visionaries see in broad strokes but implementers see in tiny pieces.

Conducting your assessment prior to going into business tells you whether you are a visionary or an implementer. Visionaries can see the whole picture of the puzzle before it is put together. Implementers have the tenacity to put the tiny pieces together. The big picture of visionaries starts the planning process. Truly successful visionaries get little implemented. Frustration usually develops when visionaries work with implementers. If visionaries do not get out of the way, nothing will get implemented. It is the implementers who get things executed.

Visionaries need good implementers for success

In family and small businesses this causes family members to align against each other in favor of those with similar styles. Visionaries and those who carry out the implementation do not see the same priorities do not speak the same language. In a vote visionaries will side with other visionaries. On the other side will be those who implement.

In the board rooms of America conflict arises between visionaries and those who implement. The dialogue resembles the tension between a budgeting department and a marketing or creative department, where one focuses on cost limitations and the other focuses on expansion of creative ideals.

In the corporate board room, visionaries should leave the room after presenting their vision, but continue to oversee the project from a distance. They only get in the way of those who have no vision but can perform the meticulous task of realizing the objective.

When similar conflict takes place within small businesses it hampers the ability of the business to expand and grow beyond the start-up phase. The visionary who sees the dream must step aside to allow those who implement it to bring it into reality.

True visionaries do not want details. They refuse to seek instruction and are hurried in their decision making process because they have already envisioned the process and know the next step. Implementers include entrepreneurs and teachers, who are unhurried, good listeners, and require answers to all their questions before they buy. They also require time to think.

Advancement in business requires both on a team. Few leaders are balanced as visionaries and implementers. Sharpening both edges of your emotional and intellectual intelligence helps you to be more tolerant of both.

Why would a leader start in business but then resist, procrastinate, and sabotage to keep from doing the work necessary to be successful; then wonder why there is failure. When your results do not reflect the effort you put in it indicates a blind spot. Look for inconsistencies indicating that what you say you want is not what you really want. Maybe you are not honest with yourself. Sometimes business decisions pull against personal convictions. This makes it hard to remain committed to one or the other. Another reason could be that you need a leader with a different style to compliment your leadership style. A primary reason to analyze yourself and the business is to prepare for an unexpected storm so that when you face the dilemma, you can make quick effective decisions.

The actions of one small business owner revealed that she was a visionary who opened the business but her attempts to implement were causing her to fail. Her actions reflected what seemed to be obvious blind spots to others, but not to her. If the number of customers who came in the door was her measure of success then she was successful, but if money was her measure of success, she definitely was not. Customers entered the door of her once thriving beauty salon, but because of her difficulty implementing they left before she could serve them.

The beauty business is one that women will always support. The owner had a viable vision and was spending money for marketing to promote the business and working longer hours to keep the business open appearing to accommodate her customers. However, the business was suffering financially. The owner brought in another beautician to work another chair. That's when the blind spot became clear.

When women want to look good they don't care if they have to visit your business in the middle of the night. This was especially true, that Sunday morning, a few days before Christmas, women wanted to look good for the upcoming holiday. They didn't mind missing church or getting up early for an appointment even if it meant staying there all day.

There was a drastic difference between the two operators. The new beautician knew her customers. She was up early, ate a healthy breakfast and started working at the crack of dawn. Unlike many beauticians, she engaged in very little social conversations with her customers. She worked so fast there was little time for social chatter. She was too busy making money. Customers were out of the chair and paying their bill before there was time for uttering trivia. Her objective in business was to give her customers fast quality service and make money.

By the time the owner strolled in that Sunday morning with her high heels clanking against the floor, there were at least five customers squirming, but still waiting patiently.

"You missed a lot of business this morning." The new beautician told the owner.

"I had to go to church and pray." The business owner responded.

"You spent money yesterday to market the business and prayed for customers, but you were not here when they came this morning. The place was packed." The new beautician, working on her third customer, told the owner as she walked by.

"If you knew all the problems I have you would understand why I had to go to church this morning" the business owner stopped to talk, fiddling with hair clamps in her hand.

"Well, I think God tried to answer your prayer this morning." The conversation did not stop the new beautician from working through her customer's head of hair.

By the time the business owner had finished defending her position the new beautician had finished styling that customer's head and was collecting the money. Periodically, the worker-bee beautician raced over to lift the hair dryer to check or send another customer to the wash bowl for a quick but thorough rinse.

The owner strolled out the door to get a cup of coffee. When she came back she fiddled some more at her station. A couple of the customers who had been waiting patiently got up and went outside. If success is determined by the number of customers, there were two less customers. That was money the owner could have used to pay those bills she complained about. Still talking about how she needed help, she had not yet touched the head of hair in her chair. You could almost see her anxiety as she tried to touch the lady's head of hair.

Eventually, her anxiety became clearer. It was associated with implementing the action necessary to make money. First she blamed her appointment with God that morning for her missing several customers. Then she made her customers wait, while she fiddled for another hour. For every half-hour she worked, about an hour was spent fiddling or conversing with people in the shop. Her customers, who wanted her to hurry up, were as anxious about her working as she was about not working. You could see the stress on their faces.

The owner was a visionary not an implementer. In her mind she had a clear vision to start the business. Yet, inflexible and uncomfortable in her ability to perform the day-to-day minute duties necessary for her vision to take form, hesitation kept her from executing her dream. This was a blind spot she could not see. What she could see as a visionary, stopped short of implementing. There was no elasticity, no flexibility in her belief or ability to consider other options of making money, like simply adjusting her church schedule to another time. She believed she could only worship on Sunday morning and it had to be in church. Her belief system was a blind spot that stopped her from making money. Failing to assess, she did not understand that she could have easily hired more operators to run the business. She then would have valuable time for planning a higher vision for the business or going to church. The blind spot she could not see was that attempting to operate the business was what kept her from making money.

Leaders who have failed to assess and understand their dominate leadership style as a visionary or an implementer will not generate the necessary rhythm to achieve true success in business. Imbalance negatively impacts the bottom line of the business. Ultimately imbalance develops in other areas of your life.

Focus

A main ingredient to excel is the focus of your energy. Giving people with drive and positive energy a tangible vision produces enormous results. The ability to focus consists of concentration and vision. Consider chess masters who can see twelve moves ahead on the chess board. Before they make a move, they remove all obstacles in their mind so that their vision is clear. Having focus, drive, and energy makes a significant difference in your ability to give your vision legs and get it implemented.

Develop a process

A process is a series of steps designed to give structure to producing results. An organization is only as effective as its processes. If your business is manufacturing, how well do you understand the manufacturing process for your products? Do you have a process for ordering, receiving, tracking and monitoring inventory. Do you know the suppliers for your parts? Do you have a process to insure your risk, protect, manage, and back up your data, receive and deliver communication and to allow your mobility without interference?

When an unexpected fast ball is coming, some people squint and close their eyes just when they need to see. In business fast balls come every day. Planning and preparation gets your business ready for the fast and the curve ball. Analyze your vision to see what unfolds in daily life. Anticipating and charting change prepares you for the unexpected. With experience and planning the invisible becomes visible and less frightening.

Make a commitment

Your success in business will come partly because of your determination to stay committed. Anticipate the challenges that you will face. These challenges will strengthen your character. Allocate time and adamantly refuse to allow anything to cause you to lose that focus. Knowing your "Why", your deepest desire to achieve gives you the ability to focus. By continuing to concentrate deeply, through even your worst crisis, keeps you committed and on target.

Align strategically

In golf you re-align your position before each stroke. In business it is good practice to re-align as you achieve each goal. When you encounter obstacles, stay in alignment with your target. Despite detours, keep advancing forward.

A road map outlines the direction towards your final destination. Align the mission statement of your business venture with your inner values. Knowing your inner values and clarifying your mission makes it easier to achieve your primary objective. When your thoughts and actions are in alignment, you have fewer distractions, less work is required to carry out each step, and your drive takes you further. As your beliefs become more congruent internally and externally, your actions become more natural and require less rehearsal. There will always be adjustments to your aim and direction, but only as needed.

Success in business and the rapidly shrinking global world demand that your people skills be sharp and aligned with the objectives of your business. Focusing solely on strategic skills without attention to interpersonal aspects of relationships is equivalent to a company producing a product without a marketing plan.

The policies and procedures of an organization set the expectations for the team. When the intentions of the entire team are in alignment, efforts flow more smoothly with freedom of movement allowing the team to advance more rapidly. Aligning team members and the goals of the organization helps team members to perform better. The energy of everyone on the team contributes toward making progress, but the leader sets the pace. When my team was unproductive, I had to check my pulse.

Be flexible and stay grounded but not earthbound

The key to perseverance is to continually keep trying despite some bruises. Continually get back-up and try again or attempt another way. The process of persevering is long and arduous but it slowly develops into growth. Experiencing a fall helps to eliminate uncertainty of what it feels like to fall. Growing through this inner process is something that cannot be delegated; only you can do it. Each person has a unique recipe. A cake that is put into the oven has to bake in its own time. Your time may be different from another.

The process takes as long as it takes. It is risky to stop the baking process too soon. It is difficult to re-bake a partially baked cake.

Follow your inner voice

Be more available to yourself. Increase your willingness to simply be. Enhance your performance in areas where you are able. Contain your feelings of needing to have more in areas of your life where you already have abundance. Be more related to people in areas that are of importance to you. Use your creativity to lighten up in areas of your life where there is tension.

Balance areas of life, health, career, relationships, personal development, fun, physical, emotional, nutritional and financial goals. Make a personal shift in perspective to one that really empowers you and lets you accomplish with ease what you now want. Focus on daily habits current challenges that need immediate resolution.

Share your vision. Focus on contributions you have made. Highlight things that went well in your life and create more of those moments. Identify the times in your life when high performance and high fulfillment came together. Examine how you made that happen. Focus on things that excite you. Be curious, flexible and receptive to ideas, intuition, and insight. Don't be afraid of being led astray by your inner voice.

Add rhythm to your uniqueness

In golf, rhythm involves the free flow of your arms as they swing the club. Rhythm keeps all the movements coordinated; balance keeps you centered. Your body bends give flexibility that allows your torso to turn freely. Rhythm helps a team to flourish.

Finding a natural rhythm in your style is essential for business success. The rhythm of leadership should be a smooth, flowing tempo. Developing rhythm involves gradually accepting your own flair and excitement that adds uniqueness to your style. In the process, outside chatter that keeps you numb and dumb eventually decrease. As you find your rhythm, you become aware when something is not right. Finding your rhythm, leads you precisely to your truth.

There is a unique balance for each of us where spiritual, mental, emotional and physical merge together to form our perfect rhythm. It brings all the elements of form together into a unique individual style and makes performance more appealing.

Your inner essence guides you to that perfect balance where deeper meaning and purpose are found. At the core of the crossroad, you discover connectivity between your past and your future. There you find courage to step out of the past and gain inspiration to move ahead towards your mission.

Communicate effectively

The ability to communicate, like leadership style and emotional stability, affects team productivity. One-way communication is no communication at all. There are many roles of leadership, ranging from corporate CEO to team leader or parent. All leadership roles involve aspects of being heard. Openly communicating requires an element of trust; but also being trusted. Trust, like financial freedom, gives a feeling of security. Communication is a form of public relations, an important aspect of the business. It provides an opportunity to release feelings that keep members on different sides. Poor relations do as much damage to a business as not keeping the product on the shelf.

When your intentions are not clear, you fail to communicate; people easily misinterpret what you say. Communication is especially important when crisis emerge to pull against your mission. Know and clarify your mission, values, and your intentions. Follow them consistently.

Tolerating means allowing other points of view; especially in a crisis when a pressing situation requires attention. Don't let minor emotional scratches mount into serious bruises that remain hidden beneath the surface. They continue to grow into blind spots and may unexpectedly surface to derail your future performance. Small frustrations can grow into blind spots that cause psychological distortion in your business.

Growth can bring special challenges that stretch the seams of the business and its relationships. Effective communication keeps a flow between management, customers, and employees, especially in urgent times when contact is crucial. Communication can resolve cultural and individual differences. Effectively communicating your mission to each member of your team gives the team clear direction.

Interpersonal relationships function more effectively as listening skills are improved. A vital key to effective communication is listening. Learning to communicate with people starts with the ability to connect and listen to what they say. More important is the ability to hear what they do not say. Connecting allows you to go beneath the surface to hear what people are saying silently at a level beneath the exterior that they show. If communication breaks down, ask yourself where might I be misinterpreting what I hear?

Carefully evaluate your team

There will be situations when being an effective communicator is difficult as with my employee. I knew that listening was important.

I tried to listen but she never said anything. She continued to withhold her reasoning. Attempting to discuss the situation with her again brought a wave of hostility that hostility prevented real communication between us.

When a relationship lands in the sand trap, keep the setbacks short-lived. Do not stay stuck. That evening I took my keys from her and gave her notice that I would let her go in two weeks. Then I adjusted the schedule so that she would not work alone for those two weeks. The experience kept me much more observant of the staff and the bottom line.

Address bad news quickly

As the business environment changes, whether through expansion or downsizing, new standards and objectives need to be re-aligned and quickly communicated. It is better to know about unfavorable news quickly before it is too late. A shift in customer demographics or a downward trend of market share would be better known early than late. Failure to adjust quickly may lead to involuntary adjustments that force an organization to adapt. Challenges provide the business with opportunities to test the processes and make strategic adjustments to stay in alignment with the mission statement and core values, but also to stay apprised of new trends. Periodic assessments are good for everyone, especially when there are various departments with opposing interest. It helps to keep each team aware of the status of available or limited resources within the various departments and informed of sudden changes.

In non-urgent times, adjustments that are not necessary can always be put off until a later time. Waiting until it is too late when you are forced to make involuntary adjustments to downsize, or right size puts unfavorable pressure on a business. The more a company's policies, processes, products, or services are in alignment with its mission statement and communicated, the easier it is to adjust.

Give timely feedback

Effective leadership resembles golf because it quickly communicates clear expectations to the team. Golfers know the value for par before each stroke and that value never changes. Timely feedback allows you to strategize and make quick adjustments needed for staying on course. A golf course gives golfers immediate feedback. After each stroke and after reaching the flag at each hole, golfers know how their performance compares in relation to par. If they boggy, they immediately know their performance was less than the expectation for par.

By aiming to understand individual differences and positions, and by working to resolve them quickly, you move the team through misunderstandings that would otherwise keep it stuck.

Maintaining a successful bottom line is a benefit to all members of the organization. Timely feedback helps diverse teams to understand the mission and operate within the same standards. Being open to new ways of connecting with your team improves communication between a leader and a team.

Understand and manage conflict

Conflict, like distortion is a distraction that takes a leader's eye off the ball. Internal and external conflict keeps you caught up in mental chaos that hampers your ability to perform. To manage conflict that may arrive on your team identify strengths and weaknesses, skills, knowledge, personality, insight; along with areas of interest, then organize data and share it with your team.

Determine who benefits from your conflict. It is said that whenever there is conflict between two people, there is usually a third unidentified party hiding somewhere in the bushes. When you get advice from someone you think is a friend be sure that person is not a confidant of your competitor. The free advice you receive may come from the ranks of an opponent, designed for your demise. Your successes and your failures are influenced by many people. Be careful where you get your advice, especially if it is free.

I remembered earlier that morning hitting a ball, driving it off the fairway to the fringes of the green. It landed just beside a large tree, which obstructed my view of the flag. I wanted to pick up my ball and move it to the fairway but I could not. Under the rules of golf, executing a stroke from the wrong place causes you to incur a two-stroke penalty or lose the hole. Refusing to accept this obstacle only kept me tied to it. The quicker I embraced the obstacle and came up with a game plan to get around it the faster I could take action to move on. The best approach was to hit around the tree to a target on the fairway that put me in a position to continue toward my ultimate goal. Success commands you to persevere through what you may not like. You will likely encounter this situation again. The more you encounter something the easier it becomes. The more you succeed at it, the more you begin to like it.

Know the entry point and exit strategy of your game plan. Stay focused when an unexpected incident or a hostile opponent attempts to push you off your path. Lead with your intelligence; keep it above your emotions. You need more energy to stay focused while being dragged through life's dramas.

Like the fourteen clubs in a golf bag, within you are the tools and skills that get you through many terrains. This includes: flexibility, emotional and intellectual balance, aim, alignment with your purpose, focus, vision, good health, exceeding your standard, disciplined practice, passionate drive, effective communication, persuasion, and character.

Create a brand Develop an expertise

Branding is what you stand for. It generates a feeling, creates a connection and builds a relationship that has a positive impact in a particular field of expertise. Knowing the uniqueness of your product or service helps you establish a solid foundation in that area. Target who needs it and how to get your product to them.

Your brand is your identity. It reflects who you are, how you live. A brand makes everyone fully aware of what you stand for. It is not a temporary act. Your brand reflects the total you, whole and complete. Does your leadership brand make your environment a better place? Does harmony and co-operation reflect in your leadership style? Does your brand make you known for empowering your team or acknowledge you for a sense of integrity? Does your brand of leadership give praise for accomplishments? Consider defining your brand of leadership to reflect consistency and strength so others see values as your driving force.

Identify your target customer

Time and money spent marketing to the wrong target customer will not convert into sales. If you are working harder but making less to keep your existing customer it may indicate that you are not in alignment with your costs or your customer. Working harder is not the answer until you first attract your ideal customer. Selling large quantities of financially successful products is what makes your business profitable.

Plan and assess your ideal customer before you begin to market. Test the effectiveness of your marketing strategy. If it is not working consider whether you are using the wrong strategy or either you are not in alignment with the marketplace or new trends.

Fine tune your marketing plan to appeal directly to your audience. When you offer value to the right customer the result will leverage into exceptional business growth. Rather than working harder and utilizing resources to serve a market that is too broad. Learn to just say no to business that is not your ideal market.

When you reach your target customer with a valuable service that makes the customer feel special in some way, you gain customer loyalty. Customer loyalty helps to build brand identity, which solidifies loyalty. When people are not your target customers they shop for your products based primarily on price. Test and assess your customers just as you assessed yourself.

Stay ahead of the trends

It is a good business rule to stay ahead of the trend. This may require believing in things you cannot see. It is hard to climb ahead of a new trend, especially before you actually see the change. The challenge is that it is difficult to see change before it takes place. It is also difficult to see the big picture when you focus on a minute part of the puzzle. Visionaries and people with great foresight can see trends before or as they take place. Others see trends years after they have occurred.

Years ago companies offered one-hundred percent defined benefit retirement plans to retirees who had remained loyal for thirty years. Subsequently, the defined benefit plan was replaced with a contributory plan where employees contributed a port towards their retirement. Companies then offered to match dollar-for-dollar as much as one-hundred percent of what their employees put in his or her 401k retirement plan.

Later, the one-hundred percent was reduced to fifty percent. For every dollar an employee contributed to his or her retirement plan the company put in fifty-cents. Then, the fifty-cents match was dropped to ten percent and eventually to one percent. For every dollar an employee put in his or her retirement plan the company put in a penny. Then the IRA became the employee's retirement plan with one-hundred percent of the employee's funds contributed.

Many businesses trying to compete under tight global economic conditions now view retirement plans as an added expense that keep them from being successful. While a massive number of baby boomers (currently 10,000 a day) are retiring or heading towards retirement, the retirement fund is becoming a fringe benefit of the past, unfortunately, companies today need the monies from their retirement funds to work out a solvency package to keep the business floating a little longer or to work out a bankruptcy restructure.

In today's economic tightening, the cost of a company's retirement plan increases the price to their customers. Competitors without retirement plans can offer lower prices to those same customers. Like two golf balls colliding on the green, corporate employees who have worked many years and about to reach for their retirement may collide with the company that also needs the money from that retirement fund to keep afloat.

Companies that previously stored away a nest egg to cover employees who have been loyal over the years now have global competitors that squeeze their market share. Both India and China with over a billion people have populations three times that of the United States. They are moving to the United States looking for jobs or providing out-sourcing services and are willing to work for less. This puts financial pressures on America's work force to find or maintain a job. Greater demand from these two billion consumers is also pushing up prices.

Anxious U.S. employees about to retire are unhappily working harder for less and under pressure because they expect and depend on their retirement, while newly arriving workers from the emerging global labor force are eager to work harder for less. When you do the math, getting three eager workers in exchange for one aspiring to retire is a bargain for any business.

Companies considered too-big-to-fail are failing and entire government entities are becoming insolvent. When companies pull out, entire communities lose. Insolvent businesses filing bankruptcy lose dominant positions of leadership in the community. The impact trickles down. Pension and retirement funds accumulated over many years disappear. Nonprofit organizations no longer get large donations from these once thriving businesses. Community organizations expecting large distributions from charitable trusts can no longer rely on this source.

Unstable currencies affect business

Business involves the exchange of goods and services mostly through currency. Before currency was created a barter system was used where the seller exchanged goods and services directly with the buyer. Subsequently, various forms of currency became the medium of exchange. Currency is as trustworthy as its backers or its reserve. Currency allows more leverage. You no longer have to carry the product around you can ship it after you receive money for it. Then credit was introduced to facilitate exchange. Again this system is as stable as the trustworthiness of the people who use it. Credit allows you to get what you want today with a promise to pay in the future. The stability of this system is based upon the integrity of people's promises. Some leaders and businesses believe in their capacity to repay large sums of debt at a later point based upon their ability to generate money. This leads them to consume large amounts of debt. This system works as long as there is collateral to secure the debt or sufficient income is generated to maintain the debt. If unsecured debt mounts it strains the system. This applies whether the debt is personal, business, governmental, or global.

Many regions of the world today have debt ridden economies with strained currencies. Unstable currencies affect business in other parts of the world, where those currencies are not accepted. Currency loses its true value if no one is willing to accept it. No matter what value you put on that currency it is only good if a seller is willing to accept it in exchange for their goods. In less developed areas of Africa million dollar bills exist but they buy only a few items.

Accurately assessing your business based on new trends helps you to quickly adjust. Study your business plan, manage your debt and update your financial projections often. Keep an open mind. Just because you cannot see something does not mean it does not exist.

Form global alliances wisely

Corporations race into mergers and acquisitions to grow market share. Other companies expand to take advantage of lower costs around the world.

Forming alliances across the globe corporate giants are merging methods of operation to survive difficult economic times. As the world becomes more mobile, multinational conglomerates merge despite differences in language, rhythm and style that may cause those same partnerships to come unglued. The results of these rushed global mergers are rapid changes in demographics, diverse cultures in global entities, political scandals and corporate collapse. You never really know the team with which you are joining. After the marriage the question becomes, "Do you really know who you married?"

The collapse of major corporations throughout the world is causing a ripple effect, weakening the seams of the entire global system. Like ripples across the ocean, the impact of change around the world is being felt in local communities.

Disruptions in today's global marketplace are pressuring companies to reduce the fat, including wages, cost of goods, pensions, and fringe benefits. Change is challenging employees to be more productive for less pay. Customers with decreasing incomes search for a lower price without reduced quality.

In today's rapidly changing environment, companies can barely keep up with the rush, hustle and bustle of getting products to the market faster with more aggressive methods of obtaining customers. In business speed is an important benefit that sells. The ripple effect is that customers, employees, and companies are all experiencing stressful changes that require team play.

In global consolidations, just as in small business ventures, you face the risk of contemptuous or unequally yoked alliances. Business leaders of tomorrow face the challenge of taking over the helm and accepting responsibility for hard decisions that involve complex yet delicate issues involving unfamiliar teammates.

Many businesses and investors are taking a closer look before investing, especially after the losses suffered by some under Bernie Madoff and the mortgage crisis. Take a closer look at your partners and investments.

Corporate responsibility with today's mobility

Consolidations force you to deal with people from different cultural backgrounds, with varying degrees of mental ability, and with diverse character, but may not have the same interest. Good leadership skills become crucial.

In today's global melting pot leadership is more than owning a fleet of vehicles or having the charisma to influence a tiny segment of the world. Protecting the bottom line today means that effective leadership can no longer afford the "us four and no more" attitude of exclusion. If your frame of viewing people is confined to a narrow mentality, you will be an ineffective leader in the global business world. Strong personal prejudices leave innocent bystanders wounded. It is unwise to exclude people unlike you from your team. Those who are excluded or alienated may hold solutions for improving your team's handicap. Mental diplomacy is necessary today to avoid offending people across the globe. As the world gets smaller, choices become narrower.

In today's turbulent times it is risky to take small matters for granted. Failing to communicate outside your inner circle limits your relationships to only for a season and that season may turn into a stormy one. One day when your inner circle is no longer a shield you may long for an umbrella that spreads beyond that small circle.

In today's mobile environment, people move across the globe for work, relationships, and leisure. As people travel, they take their personal integrity and values with them. However, the cultures in other geographical regions differ. Newly arriving individuals bring different integrity standards. The border patrol never checks values or integrity while searching for a long list of other potentially harmful items.

Competing in today's marketplace requires companies through their leaders to collaborate and join in global alliances. Aligning globally, you must also develop your rhythm rather than trying to operate under the rhythm of some other entity. Merging with a company of similar style and rhythm creates a more harmonious team and, therefore, a better chance for a higher return on investment.

Golfers cannot blame the equipment and leaders cannot blame the team. As a business leader today, you walk a fine line between delegating and being responsible and held accountable. There may be a risk that disclosing what you know will lead to a short-term loss. However, the consequences of failing to disclose may have far greater consequences in the future.

Entities large and small ultimately face consequences for neglecting to monitor responsibly the actions of those within the organization. Leaders who point a finger, saying, "I didn't know," dodge responsibility by shifting the blame. Randomly shifting responsibilities weakens the foundation of a business' integrity. The results of business failure include more than financial hardship. It also leads to humiliation, depression, abuse, family break up, and community deterioration.

Create transparency

A pebble in the ocean today causes ripples for years to come. Leadership in Fortune 500 companies affects the lives of thousands of people. The threat of global conglomerates failing is creating widespread ramifications and calling for more transparency.

Hidden agendas and secret intentions lead to unbalanced accounting. The growing number of investors in the Bitcoin ignores the fact that the person who invented this complicated mathematical investment remains unknown after five years. Lack of transparency ultimately results in probing spotlights. Transparency gives the outside world, especially the government, a glimpse of what goes on inside. Even if no one is squealing today, does not mean that no one sees.

Once you reach the top evolution begins. How you arrive at the top and how well you handle responsibility will determine how long you remain there.

Prepare for unanticipated pitfalls caused by blind spots

Some holes on the golf course have landscapes where the contours of the green are slightly noticeable. You think your ball will roll right but it surprises you when it rolls left. Integrity, ethics, and morals, like the green are slightly noticeable and seldom mentioned unless a violation occurs. However, when unexpected financial discrepancies develop in huge global enterprises ripples can be felt throughout the entire global economic system.

The management team is one of the most important factors in a company's success. However being a great decision maker may not be enough to survive the competition in today's fierce business world. Environmental threats such as the weather and other harmful influences can disrupt the balance and rhythm of your leadership, especially if what you think is mutual trust turns out to be a two edge sword. Despite capability, integrity, intelligence and desire to achieve by those at the helm of the organization, still the news is filled with stories of unanticipated pitfalls and business miscarriages that cause major companies to fall off a sudden cliff.

While some leaders fail, others rotate. Staying stuck in a blame position keeps you from advancing. In golf, a rotator-cuff stretch is a hug you give to yourself, to stretch your upper body. Leaders who have emerged through adversity have done so by some distinction in their rotation. They have learned to uniquely execute bear-hug strategies that make others loyal to the team. You can expect that your leadership style will determine how your team emerges through major hurdles.

Being an effective leader requires the ability to juggle many things. The mobility of our shrinking world is rapidly bringing greater diversity into the marketplace. The more diverse a team the more likely differences will develop between team members. Your challenge as a business leader is to keep all team members eagerly striving to achieve the same business objectives. Today's competitive environment poses hazards that force you to be cautious, sometimes even with your own team. Corporate affiliations that further your agenda may go against your mission statement. Incentive clauses within business contracts that focus solely on increasing profit and decreasing costs may fail to consider adverse motives buried deep within the heart. Unstable or irrational members jeopardize their entire team.

A thorough assessment makes transition easier

Letting go of investments or members on your team is sometimes necessary, but that does not eliminate the discomfort of having to detach. Before you separate from your child by sending him or her off to college, you research the various institutions, cities, student body, and curriculums offered. Just as you would prepare to send a child off to college, anticipate and prepare to evolve your business through a transition.

The evolution of a business is also similar to baking a cake. It is made up of various ingredients. People and processes mixed and blended together to create an intended goal. When a cake is baking, you cannot tell it is ready from the outside. Only by poking into the inside can you truly tell that the baking process is complete. Similarly, you examine and assess the evolutionary process from the inside where growth takes place.

By going within, you find a perfectly timed recipe with just the proper ingredients that allow you to create a formula to perform beyond your limits and excel to greater heights. Through challenges and achievements, you are rewarded with advanced awareness that your baking process is complete.

Detaching helps you evolve

There are times when you are forced to detach from investments or certain team members. Detaching can be easy or it can result in chaos. Excessive dramas drain your personal energy and the vitality of your business. Low energy is counterproductive and stifles momentum. People stop producing when they are drained or when there is nothing left to motivate them.

Lack of production in your business indicates it is time to awaken your business with a vital transformation. Customers are attracted to vitality, not to a dull or tired business.

When the products or services of the business do nothing to help the customer it leaves the customer unmotivated to purchase. When evolution stops, the wheels of commerce come to a halt, then everyone feels the effects of the downturn.

An exodus takes place in organizations when the vitality of the entity shrinks or the clients or employees no longer find meaning in the services or products it offers. When employees find their way out the door, customers may not be far behind.

Evolution

Life forces you to evolve. One element of evolution is learning to detach. Detachment is bitter sweet. Growth is about moving on. The hard part of growth is separation. Endings and new beginnings that result from the growth process force you to the next level where you again will have to detach.

In small businesses and global enterprises, the stages of the business resemble the stages of life. Childhood represents a time when you are young and fragile. It is easy for parents to mold you into what they represent. They set the first examples. You watch their actions then duplicate what you see.

Adolescents start to search in the outer world. They evolve through life discovering the process of becoming and begin to reflect their own values. These new values may deviate from those of their parents. Teens start to develop independent thinking. They gravitate toward peers who more closely resemble their new discoveries.

Teens advance and move off to college. College graduates move to new jobs. Both require you to leave behind a comfort zone, but both allow you to grow. A part of that growth is the opportunity to leave behind things and sometimes people that are no longer useful. These experiences are good lessons in learning to detach and move on. As you continue throughout life, you will have many more opportunities to let go. These experiences of detaching provide good practice to prepare you for going into business. One of the first things you will need to learn is how to fire employees who are not a good fit for your business.

In the accumulation stage of life you focus on "having" not "being." A major trait at this stage is an outer focus; impressing and being seen. This accumulation stage is about building identity. This stage may cause you to mis-identify who you really are, which leads to blind spots that keep you from truly realizing your full potential. Evolution is a process of continual growth. Transformation causes adults to ultimately realize that what they are seeking is not found in the outer world.

Business goes through a similar evolution. Business first takes on your values. As it evolves, it discovers through your board of directors, officers, managers, employees, trends and customers new values that begin to influence the business. The business continues to mature and ultimately takes on its own independent functioning without its initial founder.

In business, detachment includes the uncomfortable task of replacing employees, officers or even board members. Understanding helps the process. Today's business climate is experiencing its own evolution. Growing global demand from emerging economies is now forcing businesses to evolve. This is sending business through a transformation.

Mistakes made contribute the most to a leader's evolution. The weakness that lead to failure forces you to strengthened your weaknesses. Most highly effective leaders have used their failures as the foundation upon which their successes were built. Being able to constructively say to your team, "We've screwed up or we need help," takes a major leap of faith and trust in your team.

When taken out of the familiar fairway of your own culture, your company must find its way back to the fairway. Flexibility and a strong professional character and corporate identity will help you to quickly adapt and make the necessary changes so the entity can survive.

Success requires you to pay attention to little things. Rapid change is easy to see, like a catastrophe, you quickly realize that a change is necessary, however, when change is slow and gradual it is easy to continue on the same path with an obsolete plan of action. Gradual change comes like a blind spot that you never see. Leaders who quickly recognize ineffective strategies and make rapid adjustments can move forward without losing too much ground.

If there is any indication that friendly alliances may be turning hostile, don't disregard the warning. Make quick adjustments to protect your business interest. The time it takes to adjust could be the time it takes to fail.

Circumstances can drive you to find your purpose

"You're fired."

This was not the finale of a reality show. It was the reality of my life. Devastated, I wanted to burst out the door in a rage. The paralegal had scheduled me to be in two court rooms at the same time. Although I performed well and won the hearing in court room number one, I had failed to appear in court room number two. That made the judge furious, so the firm got a nasty call.

Failing to simultaneously appear in two separate court rooms on different sides of town created a blind spot. How could I be in two places? Being let go was especially crushing because I had given my very best. When blind spots come it does not matter how advanced you are in your leadership. It is not easy to know when you will collide with a blind spot. There is no warning, you never know.

I moved on thinking I had left the pain behind until I came in that Monday morning to learn that the partner at my next firm had disappeared with his case load over the weekend. That ended the 800-case project we were working on. Financially, I lost my job and salary, but I felt like one of Bernie Maddoff's clients who would learn he had stolen all their money and a part of their soul went with it.

Unemployed, I packed up my law degree, walked out the door stylishly dressed, confused about my purpose. Circumstances beyond my control left me sitting in my car at the intersection. Not sure where I was headed, not knowing where I was going, I drove away, but the car was driving itself.

This lost position forced me to dig deeper for my purpose. That search took me on a journey deep within. There I found myself entangled between two parents. I thought I knew myself, but going on that journey revealed all kinds of wild emotions I never knew were lurking in dark corners like blind spots. It took that painful detachment to start my awesome transformation.

At a crossroad I couldn't find the reasons that brought me to this abyss. It was the opportune time to find some different options. Longing for a meaningful purpose led me to that point where my mother and father's paths crossed.

From falling to flying

To eliminate anxiety is to lessen confusion. This requires going through that initially anxious ride and continuing to ride. If you want to accomplish great dreams, if you want to soar, you have to expose yourself to risk. You have to take some falls. You have to go to the core of the pain and discover what processes are incomplete. The discovery process helps you find your "Why"?

Success requires you to complete the incompletes that cause blind spots. Move through them. The alternative is to give up your dream. Regrets form blind spots that you look back on and wish you had made a different decision. Regrets are the things that you vividly remember. Looking back in retrospect you have the vision to see where the road detoured, but you took the "other" path. When you realize it, take your best shot to bring yourself back to the fairway. Life may not give you another mulligan to re-play that shot again. Your choices give you options of different ways to get through. Have the courage to suffer through the temporary pain of an experience, otherwise you take the low road of quitting and giving up on successfully accomplishing your dream.

Giving up on a dream waiting to be realized will keep you awake in the night, will not let you sleep, like the seed hidden inside an acorn that will never rise to the level of an oak, that dream becomes a blind spot that haunts you constantly nagging to be fulfilled. It will take you to a dead end road in all other areas of your life;

Another step to prepare your wings to fly is to go back and assess to find the weak spot where something is incomplete, then taking the necessary action for completion to occur. This requires doing the necessary work to eliminate the emotional charge.

In your subconscious mind is a recorder with all your experiences. It holds your thoughts, all the things you have said, and the image you hold of yourself. It leads you to the mold designed specifically for you. That may mean leaving security in exchange for uncertainty. Something within tells you when it is in alignment with the mold that leads to your success.

LINK # 5

BUILD PERSONAL AND CORPORATE CHARACTER

*A leader's handicap is not knowing
your strengths and weaknesses*

"What's your handicap?" The guys ask standing around the water cooler. They are looking at me waiting for a response.

I had committed to play in the corporate golf outing in a couple of weeks. Earlier this week I had pulled my old set of clubs out of the closet and started practicing. My plan for the golf tournament was just to get by. Now, I am frozen with embarrassment.

"Handicapped?" I reply.

They chuckle.

It seemed like a trick question to me; like asking a tennis player at the local playground, "What's your ranking?"

Searching for an answer, I found only a blind spot. All the time I had spent practicing my golf stroke at the driving range had not included attention to other parts of the game. Asking my handicap was like asking my IQ. While everyone has an IQ, not everyone knows what it is. I did not know.

Knowing the object of the game and how to achieve it is crucial. Hitting golf balls was something I did every once in a while at the driving range and occasionally on the course. My goal had not been to master my game.

I did not know the correct answer but my ego did not want to admit it. The ego always wants to look good and present the best image. My looking good and impressing others character had become my way of approaching life. It came from being born left-handed and always compared to others who were right-handed and considered normal. This caused a slight handicap that affected performance in everything I did.

Not knowing the answer, my ego may have tried to punt by saying my handicap was over 100, which would have been a bad response for someone expecting to look good in a golf game. Inwardly rattled, I felt off-balance. For a moment, my emotional side wanted to compromise the truth attempting to look good. But, I never learned how to hold a poker face. My punting skills were not much better. What I did know was how to bring myself back to center.

"I don't know," I blurted out before my ego could position me in a lie.

Like still waters of a pond, my response quieted the guys. Not knowing really did not matter. Not a chuckle was heard as they continued about their day. When you are honest, what you say is genuinely heard.

My golf handicap was a minor issue, but I continued to dwell on it. The guys forgot about it but my consciousness could not. An inner uneasiness of not knowing my "handicap" continued to nag me. It bothered me so much that the annoyance turned into motivation. That provoked me to enroll in golf lessons.

Turn your weakness into strength

My decision to take golf lessons arose from a desire to improve an aspect of my game. Eventually, through assessment and commitment to improve I was able to see other blind spots and turn my weakness into my strength. By becoming ambidextrous, with an ability to write with both hands, my skills and passion, especially, as a writer grew. Utilizing both sides of my brain also caused me to be more balanced, less emotional and more rational in my thinking.

The statements that you hear in early life impact what you later hear and how you interpret it. Lack of self-esteem may come from experiences that cause negative emotions, including hurt, greed, fear, guilt or anger or that stem from unresolved inner or outer conflict. Actions reflecting low self-esteem may lead to procrastinating or not taking action that could improve your business.

You strengthen your self-esteem through your self-talk. Enhancing your self-talk elevates your self-image, which develops behavior that is consistently aligned. Taking control of self-talk is absolutely necessary to re-build self-esteem. In order to grow into a new language of self-talk, you must learn new habits of listening and talking to yourself. You must also develop the ability to deny, push away, reject, and abandon all the negative, devaluing, sarcastic, belittling criticism that comes your way. There is no physical door you can close to shut out the negative. You have only your determinism to keep an imaginary door shut. The time it takes depends on how deeply these thoughts are engrained within you. Eventually, you began to see changes in your life. It is through your own thoughts that you gain power over the kind of information that surrounds you, and ultimately the actions that you take.

A part of your earlier assessment determined erroneous inner beliefs and other areas where self-talk needs improvement. Work to eliminate the negative and reinforce the positive. Keep constantly thinking and affirming silently and aloud. By using words that trigger pictures you bring about feelings and emotions. Your subconscious does not know the difference between an actual experience and one that is vividly imagined. Your imagination is more powerful than the reality that you see. An example is how actual events that you experience do not recur over and over, yet, your imagination has the power to replay them many times.

Through dedicated efforts your weaknesses become your strengths then expand to the business and employees. Applying positive self-talk while in the presence of your employees helps to elevate the messages they hear and their actions in your business. At the end of the day what your employees hear over and over is what they spend time contemplating. It impacts their future success or failure and that of your business. Positive action by employees leads to positive results and improves the self-image of the business.

You can create a powerful reality by adding vividness and passion to replays. Eventually, more positive statements begin to elevate your self-esteem. Slowly, you began to see changes in your life and release yourself from the negative influences of others. Ultimately, these replays will begin to heal the pass and reflect your new reality.

When an employee does something wrong, do not linger on it negatively. Analyze the pros and cons. Ask for input from those involved then quickly resolve it without leaving a foul odor behind

Taking golf lessons furthered my technical skills including: grip, stance, pivot of my feet, rotation of my torso, and alignment with the target. But when I evaluated the bottom line, my enhanced self-talk did more than any lesson.

Business integrity

The principles of integrity that apply to leaders also apply to the business. Around the time of the prospering 1920's, the law determined that a company is a person. How could this be since people have a conscious and integrity, but the same could not be said for a company?

Although a company may be a person for legal purposes, it can only lie or commit crimes through the people in the company. It cannot analyze because it has no brain. It has no guilt, regret or inner feelings because it has no heart. It has no conscious to know right from wrong. Actions of a company can only be taken by its founder, board of directors, officers, employees or other representatives. A company can be found to have integrity or guilt, but it must exist through the actions or omissions of the people within it. Therefore the soul of a company exists through its representatives.

A new trend is emerging today that extends the wrongs and omissions of representatives to the companies. The companies today are being charged with crimes for actions of its representatives.

Business consciousness comes through its staff. Manipulation that takes place in a business comes through its leadership or representatives. As the owner of a business you are its conscious and its soul. Through you, and the people you employ to represent the company, a business develops not only style and rhythm, but also soul.

A company takes action through its people. Sometimes when people feel fear or a need to protect they lie to defend themselves for actions they have taken. Your character gets called into question as a result of your actions but then your company is dragged into the matter because you utilized its resources.

Each day in business brings new and unexpected encounters. You often find yourself standing at a fork in the road, challenged by conflicting positions with no easy solution.

Proceed with caution rather than taking unnecessary risks to expedite the flow of business. Taking short-cuts may improve only the appearance but not the reality of the bottom line. Your inner conscious helps you to know right from wrong. When an issue conflicts with your inner sense of right and wrong, use that inner sense to make the best decision. Remember that as its leader any decision you make will also represent your company. When you courageously apply integrity and emotional intelligence, the truth is easier to disclose.

Operating on the fringes of your integrity adds risk to the company and adds pressure to you. Inner turbulence signals inconsistency. In the end, it may be easier to shut out outsiders than to stop the thorns of your conscience. Inner feelings of guilt and regret do not exist for a corporation, only for its leaders and staff. Long after people have forgotten, your conscience is still with you.

There will be sharp bends, while executing your game plan, however, align your mission then use your unique rhythm and style to execute a game plan with integrity that works best for you and the business.

Protect the character of your business

Take precautions to ensure that manipulation is not taking place in your blind spot while you are attending to other things. Keep it from interfering with the relationship between your customer and your business.

The mission statement and business plan are carried out by the staff. When personal actions are contrary to your mission statement inconsistency develops in the business.

The terrain in business and golf is constantly changing around you, but the values within you remain constant. Business, like golf is easier when you can carefully consider and analyze each new position after execution.

Internal peace in your organization is a signal that your integrity is consistent with your values. Different paths may lead you to the same outcome but having clear intentions to support your action leaves little room for doubt. When boundaries shift, clarify values that no longer define you.

In decision making, whenever possible, remain committed to your priorities, even if it means a short-term loss. Strong convictions and prioritized values make decision making easier. Remember, what is gained by crossing the boundary of the company standards may eventually cost the business substantially more.

A customer purchasing a properly designed product expects a long-term relationship with the product. If a manufacturing business manipulates the degree of that quality, contrary to its business policy, it shortens the length of the relationship between the customers and the product. Customers are forced to purchase another product sooner than they otherwise would. Your business may score a point by turning over an additional sale sooner than it otherwise would, however, rather than scoring a point, it could also suffer a penalty, if customers take their business to a competitor with better quality.

When you purchase a product, you expect the label to accurately disclose what is inside. Decisions based on an inaccurate outer wrapping keep the customer from having a true experience. Stretching an object causes it to lose its shape and its power. Stretching the truth also reduces your power and that of the company and business, especially if it crosses a legal boundary.

Penalties in business and golf

Generally, in business, penalties apply only if you are caught. When you go beyond established rules, you risk that a penalty may be imposed. The game of golf, on the other hand, expects you to impose a penalty on yourself even if you are playing alone. It is a challenge to impose a penalty on yourself, especially, when you are the only one who knows. Playing golf alone gives you opportunities to know your character. You have the option to lie about your score, when it really does not matter.

In golf, a hook shot sends the ball to the right because the club face is not straight at impact. If you hook a shot too far off the fairway, you're in the rough. In the rough alone no one will know unless you reveal it. You may hide it within but you carry the baggage around.

The actions you take when no one is looking become habits that you practice in general. If your actions cause your honesty and integrity to be questioned, it causes trust in you and the business to deteriorate. This can have a major impact on your leadership. After considering the risks, listen to your inner voice, and execute when you feel the situation is congruent with your integrity and leadership style.

Like a personal set of golf clubs, integrity is very personal to each individual. An accurate assessment helps you to know when something does not fit properly. If you choose to work outside the boundaries of your principles, others may not know, but your conscience keeps accurate score.

Eliminate baggage

When you are not straight with people you get hooked carrying baggage around. A decision made with a clear conscious rewards you with freedom and flexibility to lessen your baggage. Each situation gives you a new opportunity to lead. Character hangs around to nag when your actions leave questions about whether it was the right thing to do.

It does not matter that there is no one around. When you face a penalty, do not get stuck. Take the penalty, but keep your momentum moving forward. In golf, you can always recover on the next hole.

Truth and reality are widespread and abstract

Business values of entities in emerging markets have unique styles and different rhythms from companies in other parts of the world. A person's integrity, morals, and ethics depend on what elements make up truth in his or her geographical region of the world. Within corporate America, companies are challenged to beat street estimates to maintain their stock and market values.

Boundaries of corporate integrity become less visible as more companies merge across the globe. Global joint ventures are bringing together partners with different values. While they strive to reach the same goal, their methods differ. Different policies, laws and cultures attempt to merge. One culture legally greases the wheels of commerce, with payments under the table as the normal course of doing business. That same act in another culture is a clear violation of the law. Legitimate payments in one region of the world are called blackmail in another. This cultural changing of the guard erases legal boundaries in countries where those policies and laws do not apply. As a result of today's global transition leaders are learning the tricks of other trades.

Executives are moving across the globe, learning recipes for cooking the books. Behind mirrors hide the reality of financial illusions that appear to be real. Some of the rules that applied in the past no longer apply in today's global market place. When leaders from one culture take their leadership to a different culture, it shifts the alignment of policies and integrity from black and white to gray. This also causes the organization's standards to shift.

Build a strong corporate identity

You may not anticipate it now that your business will be crossing a bridge but plan how you will get back across any bridge you may encounter in the future. CEO's today must lead with their heads and with their hearts. When balanced, you will make a better leader. No matter how great a leader you have been or whether you reign at the height of your leadership, you need the insight of your inner knowing to warn when the risk or winds of loyalty are no longer blowing in your favor.

Great fictional and non-fictional leaders in history failed because they forgot the simple things. A tiny bug brought down the mighty warrior Alexander the Great. Samson, the strongest biblical character, was weakened by deceptive pillow talk.

Even with the greatest ability to persuade, your influence may gain admiration from many but disdain from a few. Remember, it only takes one for disruption.

The corporate soul

Bringing your deepest and most sacred human energies to work digs a path to the corporate soul. Meeting demands of the workplace and the inner needs of the worker, the business is able to attract and engage the best that workers have to offer. A corporation's soul awakens when individuals within the business are truly alive. When work becomes a direct expression of one's values the business develops a dynamic soul.

LINK # 6

KNOW THE SCORE

What initially felt like degradation around the water cooler turned to motivation that inspired me to really develop my golf game. Taking golf lessons I learned that a golf handicap is an average of your golf scores. That average is designed to allow golfers of different abilities, whether professional or amateur, to compete on equal terms.

The process of developing a handicap is like riding a bike. The only way you develop is by actually participating in the game. Golf's handicap system placing everyone on equal par, effectively compensates golfers with less skill. This is an area where golf and business part. Businesses cannot afford to compensate leadership for lack of skill; it ultimately impacts the bottom line.

Knowing your handicap in golf gives you a number by which to measure your performance. You can only develop a handicap by playing the game. Through lessons and application your game begins to improve.

Similar to a golfer's handicap, business leaders need a way to measure their performance as they carry out strategic plans. Using either a business plan or a meticulously calculated feasibility study you apply exact measurements to a situation. Then through experience you are guided where and when to adjust to stay aligned with your future goals. What makes you better comes about through experiences that apply vigorous training, proper techniques, and dedicated practice.

Set accurate measurements

It is important to monitor the score card regularly. Periodic examinations help you in monitoring progress, measuring and planning. On the golf course check your map periodically to determine the contours of the path ahead. In business, you check your business plan before you execute. Keep track of your objectives. Study what obstacles lay between you and your goal. Then decide your approach.

Like the different holes on a golf course, each day in business, you face a new and different landscape. In business you experience various people in different moods. Accurate planning helps you anticipate the divots and potholes ahead. Spending ninety percent of your time preparing and practicing your skill allows you to spend only a fraction of your time in the execution and follow through.

Time is one form of measurement. It was created to measure seasons for reaping and sowing to organize society. The planting season in business is a time for preparing the business plan. The nursing season is a time to implement the plan, then, comes the harvest time when you reap the rewards. Without time you have no way of knowing how to allocate resources. In business, properly allocating resources is necessary because resources, such as time and money, are limited. Allocation gives structure to how much and how resources are best utilized in your business or investments. Measuring difficulties may arise with investments such as the Bitcoin where it is unregulated and no one knows exactly who or how resources are allocated.

The 80/20 rule in business is another method of assessing and allocating resources. Under this rule it is not wise to spend eighty percent of your resources for what amounts to only twenty-percent of your total return. When you fail to measure, you tend to violate the 80/20 rule by wasting eighty percent of your resources to satisfy only twenty percent of customers. This is an ineffective utilization of limited resources because the investment does not justify the return. As you assess your business and investments keep tract and monitor your return on those investments.

Winning is a numbers game. The more times you play, practice and perform the more opportunities you have to get better. Practice requires sacrifice of your time or time you spend with others. Success in business requires balancing business with relationships or family. Allow yourself time for fun, balancing work time with play time, but when the road gets rocky focus more on your business goals.

Keeping score means learning to delegate

Keeping score requires juggling many things that go on around you. As the business grows you must delegate responsibility by hiring more staff, contracting or out-sourcing. To delegate effectively start with measuring the method, quality or standard you want against the results you want.

On the golf course you always know the expected standard, even before you start to play. In business know the need, opportunity, or objective that you want and when it must be done. Know the capabilities of your support team. How far are they capable of stretching? What would challenge them or be too difficult for them? In the same way that you monitor your support team you want to examine the expertise of your professional teams, those you rely on and pay for their informed information. Know the specific area of expertise of your experts. Check up on their results. Get a second opinion, if necessary. Learn how they arrive at their results. Establish good communication and effective controls for your operations, employees, and outside contractors. Create checkpoints at which you monitor progress. While your monitors may differ for various staff, vendors and servicers, exclude no one. Do not assume that because professionals charge a fee for their expertise, you do not need to monitor and track their performance or that your partner will never swindle you. Set accountability guidelines for completing work, and monitor achievements. A check-and-balance system helps monitor and maintain equal balance in the finances. The results you obtain at each checkpoint tell you whether further monitoring is necessary. Know at what point you will "step in" to intervene if necessary. "When necessary" means that no matter how much you care about the person, or the relationship, the business is facing a serious issue that needs attention. Once stability is regained you can resume delegating.

Measure often – monitor regularly

Measurements help you know where you need to improve. After each hole on the golf course you tally your score and record your gain or loss. In business your gains and losses should be recorded just as regularly.

Assessing resources and measuring return more frequently helps you to discover blind spots sooner. Tracking the numbers in business is important to monitor the score. Tracking helps you to maintain your costs. Without systematic controls your costs run rampant, which negatively impacts your bottom line.

Initially, or right after a crisis, it is better to monitor financials and operational processes much more regularly, even several times a day. As time passes with success in the numbers and the results, monitoring can be done less frequently. Control is necessary, but it cannot be too rigid; there must be balance. Over-emphasizing bottom-line results may be an imbalanced approach for a company during a time of crisis. Flexibility and emotional intelligence may override price in a major crisis.

Your map in business is your business plan, which lists your goals and objectives. It is similar to your map of a golf course listing each hole and flag. Don't wait till the end of the year at tax time to determine whether your business made a profit or loss.

Control the ego

The ego likes to fill you with pride telling you how well you are doing and how successful you are. But the ego does not measure by calculations, it measures by feelings. Emotions, both positive and negative, can be easily chased away by opposing or stronger thoughts that pay a visit and occupy your mind. Since emotions are constantly shifting, allowing thoughts to be ruled by emotions is risky. Your performance could become very inconsistent.

Unconcerned about analytical details, the ego tricks you into vague investments or tells you that you have practiced, planned, or studied enough. However, when you experience a mishap the ego is the first to judge and criticize your results.

Do not let the ego trick you into believing that success will come easily without sacrifice, without understanding, without risk. It takes mental effort, hard work and may take coaching to develop a stable golf shot. The same applies in your business and investments. Be open to instruction from others who can help. Being open to learn what you do not know, allows you to improve your weaknesses.

Comparing the rules of golf to leadership strategies, many of the same principles apply. Par in golf is structured for you to measure how far you are expected to progress in your training and performance. Understanding these dynamics and applying them lets you focus on the leading edge of the golf club at impact. This measurement can also be applied to business to improve your business skills and give more focus to solid execution, especially in decision making.

When you reach one goal pause to reflect then anticipate your next challenge. The scorecard in golf is a barometer to gauge whether you are still on target. Both business leadership and golf require continual measurements to gauge whether you are on track.

Expect a progressive return on investment

Sales in my first year of business created an initial barometer for how much I could sell. That figure became the expectation, like par in a game of golf. Later, when I wanted to grow, the expectation I had created was difficult to change. Year after year stagnant sales continued to average that first year's sales. Additional marketing and other measures did not change the sales. My business was not responding to excessive efforts to generate more revenue. Then it became apparent that the business performance was congruent with the way I saw the business. First, I had to change the expectation

I had concretely set in my mind, otherwise, nothing would change. An image you create for your business, if too limiting, can generate a future constraint. Until that image is changed business performance will not exceed it.

Learn to read financial statements

In today's turbulent business environment creative accounting poses a threat as once successful companies struggle to survive. Functional accounting details who is providing the dollar, what type of income it is and why it is being received. Creative accounting on the other hand is abstract. It leaves room for various interpretations and may create a blind spot if regulators take a different point of view. Those who criticize business and government measurements as unfair may fail to accurately assess the outcome of attractive looking alternatives. Accurately documented figures are important to tract your financial score.

The primary components of the financial statements are the balance sheet, income statement, and statement of cash flows. Other important numbers include, annual sales volumes, annual sales growth, and return on sales or investments.

Balance sheet

The balance sheet portrays the financial strength of the company. It shows what the company owns and what it owes on a certain date or end of year. A balance sheet in business could be viewed as the equivalent of the initial balanced stance in golf. Without an initial balanced stance golfers are likely to become unstable, sway, or lose alignment with their goal. Golfers maintain a strong and steady stance by keeping the balls of their feet firmly secure as they pivot. Balancing the assets and liabilities in business is just as important to keep the business steadily moving forward.

Income statement

The income statement reflects how the company performed during the year. It shows whether operations resulted in a profit or a loss. Income and sales may not be the same. Income coming from the sale of assets is not a sale to a customer. If all income is from the sale of assets, it means that no customers are buying your products.

Generating income does not mean your business is generating profit. Profit is what remains after all expenses are paid. Millions of dollars in sales is good, but good financial management is better. Poor money management results in losses no matter how much a business generates in sales.

Two of the biggest costs challenges facing businesses today, besides payroll and inventory are insurance and taxes. Insurance payments may include worker's compensation, hazard insurance, liability insurance, property, life insurance and health insurance. Business taxes may include sales taxes, income taxes, intangible taxes, property taxes, excise taxes, capital gains taxes, payroll taxes, or accumulated earnings taxes.

Business taxes may include, among others, sales taxes, income taxes, intangible taxes, property taxes, excise taxes, capital gains taxes, payroll taxes, or accumulated earnings taxes. Payroll taxes, including 940 and 941 taxes, are blind spots for many businesses today and are the quickest ways that businesses get into trouble with the Internal Revenue Service, when these taxes are not paid. This is because some contracted financial service managers or bookkeepers do not include these taxes in the contract for the services they provide. The business owner thinks these taxes are being paid, but later learns that they were not. These are the taxes that stay alive to follow the business owner even if the business dies.

When you pay companies for contract services, check the solvency of the companies, especially if you pay in advance or yearly for services to be rendered in the future. You want to insure that they do not become insolvent leaving you with no service or coverage after making advance payments.

Certain assets of your business, such as equipment becomes worn and eventually needs to be replaced. Each year a deduction can be taken on your business tax return to represent the amount that asset has deteriorated during the year. This deduction, called "depreciation" does not require you to spend cash, yet allows a deducted on your annual income tax return. Without reducing your cash you lower your taxes.. The IRS allows you to take more depreciation in the early years of an asset's life. This is called accelerated depreciation. Accelerating current depreciation on your income tax return is a recognized method to reduce income taxes today. This may, however, become a blind spot in the future when you sell the business and have to pay back the excess depreciation taken in earlier years.

Break-even point

Break-even point tells you the exact amount it takes to make a profit on each item sold. If you do not know your break-even point, each product that you produce may be costing your business more money than what you are making when you sell it.

Your business may be operating at a lost to produce and sell that product. You need to know how long your liquidity will allow you to incur losses.

Statement of cash flows

The statement of cash flows reports the movement of cash for the period. Thoroughly analyze your financial statements, including footnotes that provide more detailed information about the balance sheet and income statement.

Refine your goals often

Evaluate your overall planning process. Set goals, make decisions, identify resources, assign responsibilities, specify and evaluate options and create timelines. Don't forget to measure, follow-up and update your financial barometers often.

LINK # 7

UNDERSTAND THE PEOPLE GAME

A successful business needs a supportive team to carry out its strategic plan. The ability to keep the team working towards a mutual goal is crucial for a leader. Teams work best when people work together with a clear aim and clearly articulated organizational goals. Leadership based on integrity and respect can effectively align members of the same or different cultures in successful strategic business ventures.

Hiding keeps you handicapped

Employees with weak or unclear standards place your business at risk. Business functions best with clearly defined, measurable standards that have been communicated to the entire team. Without the ability to know what is in the hearts of your team, your vision and ability to plan are limited. When employees fail to communicate you are at an even greater disadvantage.

Knowing the internal motives of members on your team is crucial to allow you to plan accurately. A mistake of judgment in hiring or regarding your customers can cost you resources. After spending your time and money, you discover action that is not in the best interest of your bottom line. This requires you to make quick adjustments then more resources are necessary. Loss of time and money you can recover, but from a major catastrophe you may not. This could expose your business to insurmountable risk that could interfere with your business survival.

Failed relationships lead to derailed teams

Relationships work like a bank account. Negative encounters cause a relationship to be stressfully overdrawn. Withdrawals that deplete relationships include not meeting expectations, having negative attitudes such as arrogance, insensitivity, being inconsiderate or too aggressive. These attitudes especially impact a business if the customer is the one who suffers. Other leadership styles such as being self-absorbed, not being present, being inflexible to redirection, too aggressive, or imbalanced may lead to the same failed relationships in your personal life as in business.

Force reduces the lifespan of relationships:

The situation with my employee arose from a blind spot that I never saw coming; nothing I could have planned for. That employee's actions interfered with the natural rhythm of my team. The outcome would have been very different if I had used force to manipulate a certain outcome.

In golf a forceful grip maintains tension. It negatively impacts the outcome. Likewise, relationships built by force destroy natural rhythm. Force robs others of the opportunity to trust you and murders the natural rhythm of relationships. Force inhibits the natural binding ability of individuals and reduces the lifespan of relationships. Leaders who build relationships with force take short chip shots but may later suffer consequences that prove fatal to long-term relationships. Violence buries all points of view. Short-term successes to gain narrow, imbalanced goals show a lack of emotional intelligence.

Some people do not achieve greatness because of small minded pride, or other prejudicial beliefs, along with their refusal to change. With their mind made up refusing to change, they create conflict by persistently holding on to misinformation, or forcefully imposing their beliefs on others. Force leads to violence. It robs you of the ability to develop alliances by disconnecting you from people and creates emotional distance between you.

Confusion and chaos keep people from understanding, even when they all speak the same language

Individuals need no weapons to wage war. When people harbor deceptive intentions, biases, and hidden agendas, they do damage to their team and to others around them. Taking away trust removes a vital connection in a relationship. Manipulation interferes with the genuineness in the connection between the parties. Manipulation drains vigor away from productivity causing performance to drop. This secretively covers up the truth, which leads to deception.

Manipulation and force give a false sense of power

Clinging to the past creates prejudices based on obsolete information. What worked in the past, fails as irrelevant. No matter how smart or knowledgeable they are, when uninformed leaders cling to what worked in the past, change eventually forces itself upon them.

Awkwardly performing under another's restraint takes away your rhythm. When you force people into artificial roles, it pulls weight to one side of the team's center. As individuals with obsessive desires for control and power clash, it causes conflict to escalate. Eventually, the imbalance causes the team to spiral downward.

Using force to control people ultimately creates the same unrest and resistance that develops into civil unrest and war. Each member of a team feels the conflict just as each member in the community feels the unrest inflicted on that community. Exercising force is not true power. Without collaboration, forced change results in fallen leaders and empires. Force manipulates control upon others. It is superficial power that lacks influence. Using force to gain control requires continued force to sustain that same level of control. Despite apparent gains, resources are inevitably strained. Leaders who gain advantage by brute force lack mental maturity.

Force is rarely sufficient to change behavior. The push and pull of different points of view creates extreme stress. Finagling and cajoling others lead to broken links in the relationship. Regardless of whether individuals join in partnerships or companies consolidate in mergers, the combined team needs to be free from stress that more likely pulls the relationship apart.

Rules and legislation do not change a person's heart

Thinking back on my employee, what I know is that you cannot force an employee to change. Enacting rules may change a culture's behavior; it does not change what is in the hearts of people. Similarly, force may change behavior, but it negatively affects your rhythm and leadership by creating animosity in the heart.

When you rob people of their choices, they lose trust and develop animosity. An obsessive need to control reflects an ego that suffers from malnutrition. The natural tendency of people is to be free of disempowering leadership.

At some holes on the golf course, one road leads across the water to the putting green and that same road leads back. When you cross a bridge with only one way in and one way out, plan how you will get back across that bridge. Remember, as you climb the ladder of success, you may have to travel back down that same path needing the support of those you pass on the way up.

Using persuasion to influence is more effective than force

Relationships are more successful over the long term when developed through influence rather than force. While control over other people is superficial, influence is lasting.

Whether and when a business is derailed, the energy of the leader determines how quickly it turns around. Quick action must be taken to assess the situation, then implement quick strategies to plug leaks caused by rising costs, dropping sales or other problems.

Persuasion occurs at a mental level, requiring finely tuned management and interpersonal skills. Emotional intelligence allows you to genuinely connect with people and they build trust in you. This is especially valuable when time is of the essence during a crisis when an ax is falling. Energetic leaders are able to form synergy with team members that reciprocate energy and propel the entire team forward.

Persuasion improves your ability to effectively communicate. Individuals are attracted to be on your turn-around team partly because of what is inside of you and how you use it. The seeds that you plant will harvest in-kind results. Use your ability to influence strategically to bring others into alignment with your primary objectives.

Rather than taking the easy route of excluding others from your platform or resorting to force and manipulation take the more difficult high road of learning to influence them. Develop the skill to influence through persuasion. This requires that you get to know them. Instead of focusing on the disparities between you and others, let the power of your goals move you higher. As you climb people will look up to you. From a higher elevation, you have a wider angle view.

The power to influence comes from within. Learn to understand the internal mechanisms that move people. Moving a team to action through influence requires learning to utilize powerful inner facilities. Influence utilizes persuasion that allows alliances to develop and grow.

Influence gives you power to mow through tall grass

In a hazard on the golf course changing to a club with more loft lifts your ball up and out. Similarly, using your inner game of leadership you gain power through influence that lifts your team rather than attempting to mow through a situation with manipulated force. Manipulation only creates an appearance of power that ultimately only slows down your leadership. Influence allows you to achieve great results with inner power. Meaningful and lasting change starts on the inside and works its way out. The same is true for a business. Meaningful change starts high within the ranks of the organization, then, it trickles down to the staff below.

Know the competition

Blind spots develop when you do not clearly understand your product or your target market. It is difficult to truly assess your competition. Understanding the competition includes distinguishing elements of quality and price, there may be a low end and high end customer. Products designed for a low end market do not compete against products designed for a high end market. When you clearly understand the benefits of your product or service then you can understand who else serves that same need.

Be clear on your major competitors, their products, sales volume, and market share, to help assess your competitive strengths and weaknesses. The better your assessment, the more finely you can tune your distribution channel. Consider further your strengths and weaknesses in the area of technology. Know how your products differ.

Consider the vulnerable weaknesses of your competitors and how they might respond to a new competitor intruding on their turf. Know specifically how your product benefits your customers more than those the competitor is currently offering.

Consider team disabilities and as well as abilities

In today's competitive environment, you never know the moral character of the people that you work with and hire. It does not show on their resume and may not be revealed through references or their Facebook page. You may never know their true character until their actions jeopardize the success of your business. Accomplishing your agenda may require working with people who have very different degrees of character or who operate on a different set of ethics.

Effective team leadership takes an extreme amount of strategy when team members have different cultures or business intentions. A blind spot potentially develops when a member's business interest is not aligned with yours.

No matter how skillful your abilities, your success depends on others. Many applicants who apply for positions in your company may have your equivalent academic training yet very different internal makeup. That day I learned how employee disabilities are more important than abilities. How do you assess intentions held deep alongside one's passions?

While each member may have similar educational backgrounds, each has unique motives. Just because team members went to your same prestigious school does not mean they have your same values. Picking employees is like picking products off a shelf. You read the ingredients listed on the label, like reading the litany of accomplishments on a resume. Ultimately, you happily take and purchase the product based on what you read on the attractive package. But, seldom do you know what is really inside the package. Even searching through a person's background may not reveal what is buried deep within the heart. You usually discover the truth, after you commit to putting them on your team.

No matter how prominent or wealthy a leader becomes the story of Dr. Jekyll and Mr. Hyde illustrates what happens when that person lacks personal integrity, holds a hidden agenda, and fails to communicate to both his inner and outer world.

Well-respected and of prominent stature in the community he was born to wealth and had every guarantee of an honorable and distinguished future. Yet he found it hard to reconcile what he believed was a warped desire for pleasure with the expectations held by his peers in high society. As he concealed his true self, he began to deny it. His integrity was lacking as he hid from others a simple truth he could not admit to himself.

Rather than resolving his internal emotions with intelligence, he resorted to taking a solution that made him feel younger, lighter, and sensuous. He so much delighted in how undignified he could be, the pendulum began to swing further towards pleasure. Then it came crashing back as he began to lose control. Guilt and keeping secrets about his desire for a simple pleasure caused his destruction. His community lost a notable community leader.

Team work and team building

Structuring a good team is a necessary part of a business plan. A team includes not only your employees but also your bankers, suppliers, customers, family and others. Effectively utilizing resources is an important part of building a team. This requires first identifying skills, knowledge, experiences, and other inner and interpersonal strengths. Look at what skills or knowledge you have to help the team achieve its goals and what you would need to create an effective team. Some of the skills the team will need may include facilitation skills for team building or managerial skills to reach targets and accomplish goals, or technical skills for researching, designing or writing.

When mishaps tear at the seams of your business, teamwork can mend the situation to pull you through. However, when you team with people with bad motives, even the best-laid plans can go awry. Regardless of the size of your entity, whether a small business or global enterprise, you need to know what ulterior motives of people on your team are not in alignment with your goals. Sabotage results when the internal desires of members of the team pull against those of the organization. The potential for conflict also arises when team members develop hidden agendas or withhold necessary information. This puts your leadership at risk. Your ability to resolve conflict becomes crucial.

Corporate security helps job security

There are increasing news stories of employees with access to business information leaking it to a competitor. This shows the potential for corporate sabotage and how important access to your inner processes can be. Job insecurity for employees may lead to insecurity in your business.

Efficiency in cost, improvement in quality, and increasing sales are the best job security for an employee. For management job security is the ability to bring positive and meaningful change, to rally and motivate the team, rewarding hard work and results.

Engrain progress into your business culture to motivate employees; involve them, get feed-back from them. Employees' contributions (good or bad) make a difference in the product or services' offered. They possess the potential of a vast resource of ideals and energy, enthusiasm and team work. Your direction and judgment may determine whether they use it for good results or bad.

Leverage customer service

Relationships involving newly hired employees and customers in a newly opened business require special attention. Customers expect to be valued. You deliver by providing consistent quality customer service. Employee satisfaction leverages into customer satisfaction. Develop successful techniques for interacting and working effectively with employees, especially if they interact directly with customers. Empathize with customers, work to solve problems and meet customer's needs. Understanding helps to gain and maintain customer trust, dedication and loyalty. Investing time in a relationship helps it to grow in depth. In business this improves sales performance.

Apply golf's best ball format to building a team

The morning of the corporate golf tournament arrives. As I turn into the golf resort I can see carts lined up ahead. Tension begins to build. This tournament is a company outing intended for team bonding and fun. Everyone seems so tense. My tension is because it is my first golf tournament, but why is everyone else so tense? Senior level staff seems concerned about the level of their game, while lower ranking staff, the guys are jockeying for positions near the centers of influence. This has little to do with golf; it is more about office politics.

As I approach the clubhouse, I can hear the guys discussing the rules of the tournament. The format is best-ball format. This format relieves pressure on unskilled players because it allows a team of four to each hit, but it counts only the best of the four balls played.

The team, called a "foursome," has two golf carts with two players in each. They ride the nine or eighteen holes of the golf course together as each of the four players takes a turn hitting their golf ball. Only the best shot of the four is counted. The other three players pick up their balls and take them to the location of the best-played ball. From this point all four players then hit their next shot. This structure provides three backup players, so even an amateur on a foursome team can feel comfortable competing against other foursome teams.

Best-ball format creates a powerful and supporting environment, promoting bonding among the foursome. Not always does the most experience golfer play the best ball. At times, each member of the foursome may have a best-played ball. The best-ball format lets you know the skill level of each team member very early in the game. Imagine knowing the true expertise level of team members before or shortly after your team is formed.

Spending hours getting to know your partner in your cart, while also spending considerable time with the other two players making up the foursome, allows a deep level of bonding to occur. At least one of the four players in a foursome generally keeps the team on track by hitting a ball that lands in a respectable position. While the best-ball format involves a team, achievement is still the result of each player's individual performance. When you compete against yourself, you are the only one that matters.

Using a best ball format of a golf tournament is one effective method of applying team dynamics. Under this format the entire team has one shared purpose, allowing the members to get the most out of the team and the team to get the most out of its members. All members contribute to a win-win style involving fun work and play, yet, only performance counts. Performance is evaluated by results. Regardless of skill, all team members work together toward the same objective, utilizing the best of each member's abilities to help win the game.

Best ball format structures team play to give everyone a chance to be the best. The strengths of each person are a contribution to the team's success, while no one's weakness is penalized.

Encouraging team members to compromise, recognizing their differences, or being tolerant of each other's styles is not always easy. Through performance, best-ball format reveals faults, even when team members are unwilling to admit their own weaknesses.

It is difficult to solve problems when team members are either not willing to compromise or are not tolerant of another's situation. Until they share the same experiences it is difficult for people to understand.

Imagine if business leaders developed a similar structure by arranging teams so that new members feel comfortable as they get to know the team and as their individual level of skill in the new position develops. In business, like best-ball format you win because the team wins.

Without input in the decision, I am appointed to a foursome. I have no say in selecting my team. Golf, like business, has certain variables you control while others you do not. For a moment, I feel slighted, not being able to participate in this decision.

It is a natural tendency toward leaders wanting to be in control. However, sometimes by giving up control, you gain an opportunity to grow. Growth is venturing beyond those you know. My choice would have been to golf with those I liked or those I knew best. But that would have given me—and my teammates—little opportunity for interpersonal growth.

Business sometimes places you in situations outside of your choosing. Other times life deals a hand you would prefer to change. Detours in a game plan do not prevent you from reaching your goal. Instead, they prepare you to get through what lies ahead. Instead of complaining, consider accepting the hand you have been dealt. Acceptance is an inner mechanism that gives you a measure of control over external circumstances that may otherwise cause disruption in your game plan. Choosing to accept the situation may be the best course-of-action to stay on track. No matter how different people are or how far apart their positions, there is a common denominator that can bring them together.

I experience anxiety while walking to find my assigned cart. As the foursome gather, we exchange brief pleasantries. Our personal lives and our golf experiences have few, common threads. Trying not to offend them with small talk, I allow them to continue their conversation. Initially, I remain inconspicuously present, but confidently make eye contact and smile. I gradually become a part of their conversation. As we began to play, we genuinely communicate about parts of our lives we have in common. After the guys hit from the blue tee at the first hole, all energy focus on me. "Women hit from the red marker," my partner supportively informs me. Experiences always teach the things you need to know, when you are open to learning. I learn more about the golf handicap and the system of par. At each hole, there are colored markers, usually red, white, and blue, that allow golfers of different skills or handicaps to tee off at different distances from the flag. The pre-calculated number of strokes called par functions under this handicap system so that all golfers are expected to reach the flag in the same number of strokes, called par. The golf course compensates less skilled or weaker golfers who do not hit a golf ball as far as seasoned and professional players.

As the cart stops at the first red tee, everyone stands around watching. Having the entire office waiting around in their carts to see me hit creates a feeling of intimidation. Reaching the tee of the first hole, I bend down, stick the tee in the ground, and place the ball on top. The ball rolls off the tee. I put the ball back on the tee. Feeling off center and trying to develop a smooth tempo I take a few practice swings to get the tension, kinks and knots from my joints then bring myself back to center. Tempo is a smooth flow of your back swing, down swing and follow-through. I take a practice swing with the driver.

Playing with unfamiliar teammates makes me more self-conscious about my game. There is loud chatter in my head in the form of judgments about how I look and what people may be saying or thinking about me. That causes me to concentrate less on the fundamentals of my grip, balance, and alignment.

The intellectual verbiage in my head combines with the tension in my body to hamper a smooth, natural swing. My swing is rather jerky. The club head of the driver does not touch the ball but comes so close that the ball rolls off the tee again. Since the club head does not touch the ball, it is considered a practice stroke.

I hear "Ohoo" coming from the direction of the guys. Hearing that only make me focus more within. I forget about playing my best. Instead, my focus shifts to how they see and judge me. That thought opens a floodgate of uninvited emotional guests, including intimidation. I forget to go through the motions of checking my grip, alignment, and stance, or transferring my weight, and aiming.

Comparing your performance to others causes you to doubt your confidence. Comparisons shift your focus and throw off the rhythm you need to perform with precision. Worrying about your performance affects it before the game even starts. Your thoughts shift to worrying about missing the ball before you get to the tee. This depletes the focus needed for accurate performance.

Judgments and expectations impact team performance. Anxiety creates stiffness in my body rotation. Hearing the guys' subtle sounds fills my head with negative emotions. This causes the grip of my hands to tighten. The tightness in the muscles of my arms and the locking of my wrist prevent a smooth flow of energy. Keenly interested in what the other guys in the office are thinking, I lose my focus. Anxious, I bend down, put the ball back on the tee, and quickly take a swing. The anxiety causes me to rush my execution. At the most important moment of impact, tension hampers the free flow of my body's movement. My whole body tenses, causing me to hit more air than ball. The ball teeters a few feet, which makes me feel all the more distressed. I bend and pick up my tee, then stagger over to pick up my ball. Emotions consume my energy and leave me feeling drained.

It is dangerous in business, leadership, and golf to execute while experiencing emotional tension. Speedy executions in an unstable environment can be risky. I had learned to practice proper setup before taking any action. Plan first, release emotions then execute with precision and conviction, but I did not apply what I knew. During my swing, instead of focusing on the flag in the distance, I anticipated comments from my foursome in the background.

What I heard from the voices inside my head was much worse than anything the others were saying. Hearing my own inner voices nearly dampens the rest of my day.

Knowing the rules is not enough for good performance. Despite lessons and practice, my performance comes down to what I am thinking in the moments just before execution as my club hits the ball.

While on the golf course, before ever reaching my target, I first had to imagine it in my mind. Before taking a stance or grip, I needed to have the objective of the game clearly in focus. No matter how well you learn to execute, when intellectual knowledge or skill collides with negative emotions, the latter will derail your game plan.

After my experience at the first tee, the little "I," the emotional part of me that remembered how it feels to be bruised wanted to take the easy way out by staying glued to the golf cart, going for the ride, letting my team members play the next seventeen holes without me. Then there would be no expectations of me. But the champion within persuades me that this alternative will not let me grow, bond, or release these negative fleeting emotions. Harboring these feelings for the next seventeen holes would only keep an emotional storm brewing that would cause a blind spot." I listened as the voice within continued, "So what that your individual performance was not the best do not hold on to frustration." That inner voice forcefully urged the champion in me, "Accept the pain, tolerate, persevere and endure through this minor storm."

Turning up the volume on that weakened voice helped me to hear it better and to stay in the game. I had to swallow some negative feelings of humiliation to bear the discomfort of that first hole. But, staying in the game provides an opportunity to laugh with the guys at my own imperfections.

Either physical or emotional bruises can take you out of play. Strengthening your tolerance level involves turning up the volume on positive self-talk and developing the power to resist against opposing emotional forces that pull at you. When you experience an emotional bruise, keep talking to yourself. What gives you the ability to endure and maintain control is talking to your analytical mind so it stays conscious. Your analytical mind keeps you in the game. How desperately you talk to yourself while experiencing the negative determines whether you can pull yourself up out of an emotional hazard. I had to dig down deep within myself and say, "Get up, go back out there and be a winner."

Each member of our foursome has a unique style that contributes to make it a perfect team. One member is good at driving a ball long and straight. A second member is good at chipping out of the sand trap. A third member is good on the short shot; my contribution is putting. I learned putting on putt-putt courses over the years. Putting is the final hole where the cash register rings. Since putting wins the game, the team welcomes my contribution.

Earlier at the blue tee, one of the guys drove a ball two hundred yards straight down the fairway.

"It's okay," my partner says, "This first tee is a par 5 with 515 yards from the men's tee. That puts us in good position. We have 315 more yards and four more strokes to stay on par."

In golf, there are mentors everywhere helpful in offering support and giving advice. Whether on the golf course or in business your greatest advice is the mentoring you give yourself. The more intense your self-talk the greater will be your results.

Leaders are not spectators

"You're a leader not a spectator sitting on the sidelines." My self-talk proclaims. That helps me to choose, to decide to stay physically and mentally in this game. Staying active forces me to focus on the next hole and let go of bottled-up emotions. In the same way that negative distractions took me out of the game, I use flexibility plus an assertive positive approach to alter my focus and keep me in the game. You will only grow by getting off the bench and staying in the game.

For a spectator, there are no expectations; you sit and judge but do not grow. Spectators do not have the opportunity to release emotional baggage. They only sit on the sidelines being judgmental of others. Spectators, less willing to take risks, stay within their comfort zone, looking out at the world. They criticize the creative work of others, who willingly place themselves at risk. Spectators are less accepting of themself because what you cannot accept in another you do not accept in yourself.

Laughter has a funny way of creating a deeper bond. My foursome all welcomes the humor. Laughter is a good medicine for alleviating negative emotions.

Delaying decisions and not moving on to effectively resolve issues costs more resources in the end. When caught in a bushy rough in your business, do not let painful emotions distract you and keep you there. Step away from the situation to consider a strategy to develop self-talk while you continue towards your goal. Determine the adjustments needed to get out of the rough. Keep your mind open to changes, including technical advances, new team members, or modern tools to achieve your goal more efficiently. Then play your best shot without looking back.

My emotions completely subside at the second tee when one of my team member's ball flies at a ninety-degree angle to the fairway, bounces off a house, and nearly brakes a window.

"Ouch," his partner says.

I knew what he was experiencing. Emotions of pride had reduced his performance the same way my emotions of intimidation had reduced mine. The guys were not so nice to him. They roared in laughter then ridiculed him for being "all talk" about his game. They offered cruel insults, repaying him for all the times he had been heartless in ridiculing them.

A key factor in performance is what goes on within you at the exact moment of execution. Golf forces you to be authentic. Lack of genuineness causes you to execute a strategic position that is not authentically yours and does not accurately reflect your true talent.

If your inauthentic position is not adjusted quickly, you become unstable. Swaying too far from center causes you to lose balance and fall. In business this means you fail.

Negative emotions such as intimidation, pride or ego pull from your center. Attempting to control your heart with intellect only makes you lose the ability to control your head. Feelings and emotions are like odors that spread. Near the clubhouse, the smell of popcorn spreads out on the course. The cologne of one of my team members drifts in the wind. In the same way, you can "smell" the fragrances of those around you and the smell of popcorn you feel other people's humiliation just as you feel their pride. Your emotions influence other people's performance whether you are a seasoned pro or a first-time player.

An entire team is held up when one member gets stuck in the rough

On the next couple of holes, his game only gets worse. Then he changes his approach and lets go of his pride. That's when his game improves. Making a smooth transition is easier when you change your emotions. In golf, when you are in a position of pressure, try a different club. In business try a new approach.

As I go within, the negative chatter in my head decreases allowing concentration to take place. This improves the accuracy of my stroke. With less doubting chatter from my head, my arms can swing freely. As my rhythm comes into alignment, I began to find my comfort zone.

The next hole is a short one. I feel more bonded with the team. Centering myself before hitting, allows me to keep my eyes on the ball until after the point of impact. Just before hitting the ball, I take a deep breath let go of judgments and feel a new sense of confidence. Looking up after my stroke, I watch as my ball sails toward the sky then magically drops beneath the flying flag just short of the hole, a hundred-fifty feet away.

Sometimes in business, like golf, you need to make a change. You must start within the heart of the organization, at the core. Attempting to stay in the same position or operate from the same strategic plan in times when change is needed causes you to fall further behind.

In business there will be some ineffective executions that put your leadership at risk. When the actions of a teammate are inconsistent with winning you want to discover it quickly and apply a more positive approach.

The team uses constructive criticism and recognition to enhance my productivity. To that I add my own self talk to remind me of those golf lessons, how to set up, align, focus and execute. Each stroke helps me to grow and gain more confidence. This same approach works in business.

Reasons and ways to network

Networking leverages your resources to help you become successful faster. An example is the rapid growth of digital Form alliances, partnerships, relationships, and strategic connections. They help you gain the ability to take on larger more interesting projects and expand into additional resources. With strategic alliances you increase productivity. This allows you to serve more customers, which increases income.

From an economic standpoint, alliances help your business share expenses, pursue new business ideas with less risk, and gain a financial or working partner, which reduces the financial and personal stress. Networking lets you do a better job more quickly. For the small business person a major benefit is the ability to avoid professional isolation and gain access to other networks by getting expert opinion or valuable information.

Improve networking skills

Networking skills include the ability to ask open-ended questions, concentrate on others, and show sincere interest. First get involved in the conversation. Listen to understand not to agree. Venture out to share your opinions and views, ask for help or offer assistance. With more knowledge you head towards mastery and let others know who you are, and share your knowledge and expertise. Work synergistically: to share ideas, give positive verbal support, turn problems into goals, take reasonable risks, and learn from errors. Networking allows you to develop win/win relationships. It lets you gather insider information on latest developments.

Before you network, search to find the right people. Seek opportunities. Look to match other styles to complement your assets, then, identify your most suitable choices. Be sure to follow-up with your new found contact to nurture the relationship. Longevity comes because you make room for fun and friendship. As the relationship develops resolve and overcome any concerns you discover. Develop a mission statement that becomes jointly owned by the newly formed alliance and its entire staff. Track, monitor, observe and record your strategy. Remember to share the results and the glory.

Treat the ideals of other team members with respect. This leads to a healthy style of communication. Even when conflicts and disagreements arise, resolve them without interjecting personality or emotional issues. You accomplish more results in team meetings allowing decisions to be made by consensus. When people respect you or the decisions made by you they are more likely to follow your lead and carry out your company objectives. Leverage the productivity of staff to get results accomplished. When team members work together, synergy develops and tasks get completed as decided. Long term success is achieved through problem solving and decision making.

The bottom line is that forming partnerships by understanding differences in human nature allows teams to be more diverse. This is consistent with today's global market place.

Reward your team of employees on par with their performance, especially when they birdie. The business in-turn is rewarded with lower employee turn-over. Remember that business does not reward those most deserving, by penalizing productive employees who suffer when unproductive employees pull a business down. Set measurement and expectations that penalize only those who violate policy or fail to perform while fairly rewarding those most deserving.

In business there may be times when punting is necessary, just remember that punting with your numbers can be risky. Know what is truly at stake.

Poker is the ability to bluff using a strategy to make the opponent think you have more than you have. It can be compared to manipulation. While manipulation has the potential to harm your business, knowing when and how to use it can be an asset. Sometimes knowing poker helps you win, especially if you know when to manipulate and when you have gone far enough. The skill in poker that makes you good is the ability to know combinations. Knowing what beats what and what is better requires a good analytical mind. If you allow emotions of greed or fear to take control of your logic you lose track of when to throw in the hand. When your analytical mind is in the dark, you are operating on pure ego or emotions, probably from a blind spot. You need your analytical faculties to really know what is going on around you. The ability to balance intellect with emotions is the best approach.

Giving

Communicate and align with your employees as partners, just as your suppliers, bankers, community, investors and customers, are partners. Think of them admirably, give them respect. Treat them with integrity. Success in business is attributable to a good location, but also your ability to give. Give incentives to employees to want to produce more, faster. This may come by employees knowing that your word is good. Give incentives to suppliers to deliver better quality. Reassure them that orders will keep coming. Give incentives to bankers to trust you. This may come from paying on time. Give incentives to investors who may invest in your long-term success. Give incentives to your customers to want to be loyal, endorse you and refer your products and services.

Giving helps you achieve quantum leaps in relationship building, product quality and customer satisfaction. Create innovative ways to give. Strive to be the best, just remember that in order for your business to gain the number one position in an industry or sector requires you to become a moving target, taking hits from competitors behind you and those in front of you. A loyal team is your best defense.

Success requires trusting relationships

Developing communication skills is important to effectively build trust and ultimately influence people. What is meant eventually becomes more important than what is said. Intent is elusive, yet, it is an important factor in leading people who either purchase from you or who work with you. Intuition can give you a kind of subliminal awareness to understand those around you.

Intuition guides you; as you follow, it leads you to build trusting relationships. Achieving your greatest potential comes, as you develop and balance your intuitive and analytical skills, then, use them to satisfy your entire team, including your customers.

Assess symptoms of your current and previous efforts to find flaws in your systems. Analyze the results. This helps to guide your future direction. Look for patterns and identify trends in your results that indicate common issues.

As inner guidance becomes more important, one challenge of the future will be trusting through digital transactions, where you never meet or see the person with whom you are transacting business. In fact, you assume it is a person and not a mathematical equation, where the house always wins.

Positive relations add deposits into your relationship account. This builds up trust that leverages into other beneficial assets. Emotional deposits that build relationships include, kindness, keeping promises, honoring expectations, loyalty, making a contribution, giving a choice, building a team structure, which is sensitive, considerate, creative, with freedom to take some risk, yet, demanding high standards. A successful leadership style has consistency, steadiness, and takes calculated precise steps throughout the process.

Develop a sense of community with your employees, a group with whom you feel comfortable without being a caretaker. The result is that the business makes significant progress and becomes financially successful.

Create a picture for your employees of how you want your business to look, review feedback from customers and let them know you hear. Give each employee a clear role and clearly set goals.

Close the sale

"ABC" in business means to "always be closing." Closing the sale is crucial to success no matter what line of business, including non-profits where fund-raising generates funding to keep the operation running. There are various steps to effective closing but it all boils down to developing and leveraging a relationship with the customer.

Always have new potential customers in the pipeline ready for a sale. The pipeline is filled through networking, promoting advertising and public relations. For a small business owner, you are the business so you are always marketing, even though marketing is only a portion of the business. Create a system where you spend a portion of your time servicing clients and a portion developing new business. Develop systems that can be repeated over and over. After generating interest from a potential client then bond as quickly as possible. This step is necessary for the close. Pain and money are very private topics that people do not readily disclose. It takes skill to get to the core of these topics, which are necessary to close. When your customer embraces you like a golf partner, you can leverage the relationship into business.

Help the client understand the product and benefits to be gained. This means identifying the potential client's pain, reviewing the features and benefits and showing how your product helps to make their pain disappear. Clarify issues of money and come to a mutual agreement with the prospective client about expectations. Once you help people understand the benefits to be gained then encourage them to close, but give them the freedom to choose whether to speed the decision making process.

Being a clear thinker, emotionally and intellectually balanced, helps you to become more skillful with people. Become a responsibility doer, highly self-motivated, enthusiastic and able to communicate effectively.

Being good in sales requires emotional intelligence to be tactful, courteous, cheerful, and imaginative, but also to develop a thick skin to prepare the fragile ego to take criticism, rebuffs, and discouragement; and most important to take failure in stride and keep on going.

The key to satisfying customers

Understanding customer problems requires getting inside their heads. The answer to what keeps a person up at night may not readily be apparent. Knowledge sometimes requires deep analysis.

To apply solutions that are not merely surface patches or quick fixes may require an analysis that comes from a connection deep within. Prior to making changes to your business or venturing out on a marketing campaign do an assessment of your customers, go within and consult with your inner knowing. Customers know when you care about them. Offer solutions to people's problems by doing something that you love. When they feel your passion, it lets them know that you care. Invest in what you love by providing a service that solves your customer's problems, while you enrich the lives of your employees.

LINK # 8

MASTER YOUR INNER GAME

To do something well requires a high level of dedicated practice. Education helps you learn formulas, mechanics, and theory. Growth requires consistency plus internal and external balance. Consistent practice converts into learned actions that eventually become automatic responses. Combine education with practice and knowledge to elevate even faster to a higher level of skill.

Failure and rebounding are both necessary for success

Too much too soon or not enough to complete a process of grounding and growing can cause an imbalance in a person's learning process. Your creative subconscious helps you to solve problems. Stress results from evading potential challenges. A necessary step in growing is taking off the training wheels and falling but getting up again.

Other people, neither parents nor bankers can advance you to the next level in your personal or business development. Only you can do that by first detaching from any negative belief, then going through a process constantly affirming the positive until something clicks inside that signals and you get it.

Acknowledge your own uniqueness

Your biggest challenges are your greatest opportunities for growth. Problems beyond your control force you to grow. A positive energy of achievement comes from being pushed to use your creative subconscious to gain meaningful results.

A part of growth is experiencing the pain that comes with it. When people fail they get frustrated, angry, or frightened.

Becoming the best that you can be requires endurance. Before you become a master in any endeavor, you will first experience failure. Remember learning to ride the bike you took some falls before you mastered riding.

Strong emotions emerge when people think their world is crumbling. Failing causes you to go inside. Inside of you is where healing takes place. Healing is different for each person, but it takes you through various stages. First there are feelings from slight frustration to despair or intense depression that takes you to the bottom of the pit. A part of growth is experiencing the pain that comes with it. When people fail they get frustrated, angry, or frightened.

The ego will fight furiously and sabotage to defend its identity. Normally, this is the last stage because after you stop going down you start to re-emerge. This starts the completion process. Once you can acknowledge, accept and forgive you are able to move on. Regardless of why or how failure comes about, whether from your own sabotage or from that of another, the result of failing is that you go within, gain more energy and understand yourself better. This clears a path for you to accept your weakness, that's when you begin to become better.

Lack of leadership direction is a common element for business failure. This easier road leading to failure does not require deep thought, effort, precision or perseverance. When asked what they want, many people recite what they do not want. Few know precisely what they want or more often unconsciously focus attention more on what they do not want.

Even the most successful leaders at times allow their focus to drift in the wrong direction. When interviewed after winning the 2006 NBA Championship, against the Dallas Mavericks, Dwyane Wade of the Miami Heat basketball team said what he remembered most was that he missed two shots from the free-throw line. Rather than focusing on the dynamic shots he made as a leading shot-blocker that won the game, his mind was focused on a few unsuccessful shots he missed. Worry keeps you looking back re-living the past. Dwyane Wade's thoughts were focused in the opposite direction of what he really wanted in the future (to win another championship). His thoughts may have contributed to the 2011 loss to Dallas, which in turn made him focus on winning. He then went on to win the 2012 and 2013 NBA Championships.

Failure and success or winning and losing cannot occupy your mind at the same time. In order to focus on your best shot you need to release all worry over past failures.

Failure to focus on success causes you to repeat those agonizing failures. The initial shock of failure is the hardest to accept. After the bruise, you heal and become stronger. Learning accumulates with each new experience. Keep full concentration on your goal but welcome those mishaps as part of your development.

Massive success is a result of few victories and many failures

Experience rather than avoid difficult situations. They become building blocks for developing character. When failures happen, experience them in the present. Each day practice for small victories because winning small victories transforms your spirit and takes you to greater triumphs. While working to improve accuracy, stay aligned with your target. In your many attempts there will be some failures, but you finally will have the success you are seeking. Practice with passion and focused concentration. Stamina keeps you in the game. Courage lets you stand for something.

Learning takes place in the present

Coaching is a process that equips you with the support, tools, knowledge and opportunities to develop your skills, better understand yourself and your ventures, achieve greater performance or produce desired results. People cannot do coaching it takes place only by "being."

Whether you get or give coaching, some aspect of your game improves and develops. Your most effective role as a coach is helping others simply "to be." Inner guidance comes more through feelings than the intellect. Humility is simply being you.

Planting seeds at the same time does not make all fruit ripen at the same time. Each person is unique, with their own individual qualities.

Two golfers starting from the tee at the same time using the same club and all things being equal, have uniquely different outcomes. Both eventually reach the same target. But, various forks in the road will take them on different trails. The difference is in their purpose and the effort and practice applied.

There will be some failures, but continual practice using proper instruction reduces your failure rate. On the other hand, continuing to practice bad habits makes them more engrained and harder to change. Working too hard and too long without proper instruction can have an adverse impact, because of the momentum necessary to reverse a bad habit. This is not a healthy game plan. Until your momentum changes, your energy continues moving in the same direction. If nothing shifts, the same patterns will be repeated. If your strategy is not working, the sooner you realize that doing the same thing is not the solution the sooner you can make a smooth transition to a more productive approach. Continually apply proper techniques regardless of the outcome.

Be cautious in making quick major decisions when you are experiencing turbulence. When you silence the outer noises and listen, you will be guided to your right path. It takes courage to launch out into deeper waters to follow that path. The secret to reclaiming your personal power is in discovering how to be authentic. Everyone is vulnerable in some area. That is what makes us human.

Through your assessment and ultimately your acceptance, you began to claim your power of being. Being who you really are without pretending or cover-ups helps you to accept your weakness. This gives you access to a part of you that has been hidden in a closet of your mind. By bringing out into the light the worst of you, it allows the best in you to shine brighter.

Use your vulnerability as a source of power. Design a new self-image that supports your magnificence. Realize the power of forgiveness. Discover the secret to an emotionally-controlled intellectually balanced life.

Take your game to the next level through your self-talk. Change ineffective attitudes and habits through visualization and imagery. Shift from negative to positive.

Become fully present and aware of your connection with others. Fulfill your capacity to have fulfilling peak experiences on a regular basis. Seek to gain peace of mind and contentment. Strive to achieve financial well-being. Accept your status in life as where you are presently stationed but do not let it take away from the dream you hold for where you plan to be.

Develop discipline

Lessons help you to realize how much you do not know with respect to your skills. Initially, it is hard to stay committed when your skills are quite poor. The slightest improvement gives you a reason to celebrate a small victory. Gradually, as you continue with lessons, other emotions emerge from deep within. A passion for learning begins to nudge you to go beyond pretense. Passion impacts all aspects of your life. Your desire for greater success makes you eager to improve and grow. Eventually, you want to learn, not for others but for yourself. You want to improve not just the outer appearance but the accuracy and skill of your overall game.

Between taking lessons, practicing proper skills, and networking with others in your field, you gradually develop your expertise. Whether you are practicing your game or in business, desire is an inner force that compels you to practice proper skills more often. It carries over into other areas. You begin to feel the same passion about your work and business as you feel in your personal life.

Success seems easy when you love what you do. Hard work feels like play, yet, you do it responsibly. As you commit to improve your skill, other benefits begin to emerge, including improvement in your field and expanded network with the inner circle of your industry, which expands your range of opportunities with other leaders in your field. Through repeatedly practicing your skills and sharing constructive criticism with others in your area, you grow in confidence. Eventually, you begin to reflect heightened knowledge and skill in your area of expertise.

Develop a consistent smooth flowing tempo

Focusing on your inner crossroad where your mother and father's paths cross helps you find your zone of confidence and purpose. Become more deeply focused and genuinely connected with you. In this mode, heightened senses and the energy of momentum enhance your physical and mental strength to perform at the top of your game, no matter what you are doing.

Effective business leadership is not being stagnant but rather moving forward. As you continue to practice, your confidence builds. Continual practice, regular coaching from an expert and constant attention to your desired result will crystallize over time to become habitual patterns that enhance your abilities, improve your skills, and increase your self-confidence. Eventually you will excel in performance. As you perform your best on every play, the experience and continual practice will most assuredly contribute towards your development.

Through dedicated consistent practice, your automatic reflexes will naturally develop. Practice movements that allow your arms and body to swing freely in a smooth, flowing tempo. Developing your natural ability helps to develop your own unique style. The smoother flowing rhythm and balance gives you a firmer stance in your industry.

Fully coordinating proper form, including grip, stance, rotation, alignment, and follow through during golf practice results in the same success that you get in business when you apply a firm stance, flexibility alignment and follow-through.

Drive with passion

The most effective swing in golf is not the most powerful; it is the one with the most rhythm, smoothness, and accuracy. The "drive" in golf is the stroke hit using the longest club, called a driver. This club has the biggest club head and the fastest speed designed to send the ball the farthest.

Like the drive on a golf course, within you is a similar drive called passion. Passion is the inner force that propels you toward your purpose. This inner force makes your goal, no matter how distant, a reality. Passion compels and urges you forward. It keeps you searching for new ways to improve your performance. Drive requires taking a wider stance. Widen your stance and turn on the power switch of passion by shifting your weight then energizing your execution.

Apply inner wisdom

Your inner sense of awareness warns you of unseen obstacles and gets you through roadblocks that would otherwise stop you from reaching your goal.

As I stand behind the ball on the putting green looking toward the hole, something within tells me the ball will roll left, though I can see the natural contours of the green indicating otherwise. Trusting the message that comes from within means I have to go against what appears to be obvious. I choose to take that risk. I remember that first bike ride; remembering how I had exchanged doubt and fear for exhilaration, which led to courage, ability, and better skill. The putter becomes an extension of my arms. An inner awareness enhances my ability to see and feel. Standing over the putter with my arms swinging together like a pendulum from backwards to forward in a smooth, slow motion movement, I gently strike the ball. It rolls slightly just before curving left into the hole. Following my inner guidance, then trusting and acting on it, and getting confirmation that I was right causes something to shift within me.

Execute with precision

Strive to surpass your best performance. Accuracy and speed are traits of an eagle. The eagle sits patiently perched, waiting for the right moment to execute. An eagle in golf is hitting the golf ball into the hole in two strokes less than par. At a par 3 hole, the ball goes into the hole in one stroke, more affectionately called a hole in one. Practicing calm movements rather than chaotic executions helps to develop a natural flow. A smooth tempo leads to a smoother more accurate finish.

Effective leaders study their future course of action. Yet, no matter how well they know it, they continue to prepare alternative strategies in the event of an unexpected storm. Golfers do this by analyzing the contours of the green at each hole to help anticipate the smoothness of the path ahead. In business, this is done by updating your business plan often.

Follow your inner light

As your self-esteem grows it becomes a guiding light. It helps you to persistently pursue new ventures. It helps leaders achieve their goals and dreams. It is said that high performers have a higher self-image.

This makes you question, can self-esteem be measured? If you could test yourself, how do you know whether you passed? Is self-esteem measured by the status or wealth of your family or by how much money you make? Is self-esteem a limited commodity so that when your self-esteem goes up another's self-esteem goes down? Does it make you more worthy by putting other people down? What kind of conversation can you have with yourself? Do you act in the way that you see yourself? What things do you know to be true about you?

What I have found to be true is that with concerted, conscious effort you can improve your "self's self-esteem", but you must make that change from within. Success in business requires you to be very intentional. In the same way, plan to take a strong, healthy self into your business.

Develop a pioneering spirit to bring new ideas to life. After evaluating the risk and deciding to move forward, stick with your plan. Maintain a positive vision of your future. Use your creative imagination to see the final destination. Then apply energy to your daily routine to bring the vision into reality.

Learn to trust your instincts. They help you see and sail through obstacles that are not readily visible. Make the abstract concrete in your mind. Study the problems that arise each day. Examine intimately that one thing that keeps you from getting to your goal, like peeling an onion, when you dissolve that, look for the next primary obstacle. Make this a habit that follows you, defines you and pushes you forward.

There are endless possibilities to improve image, but happy talk to yourself is one way to develop your inner self. Are you controlling your self-talk? If not you, then who is controlling it? Develop your natural instincts to guide you in making accurate business decisions. A valuable reward from your commitment through tough challenges will be when the image you have of yourself changes. Eventually, you begin to see yourself as the successful leader or business person you truly are.

Mine your Mind with images and affirmations

Affirmations are a form of self-talk. When they trigger a picture they bring about emotions or feelings. You hold the power to make them constructive or negative. Earlier when you completed your thorough assessment of your inner ingredients did it reveal a weak or strong self-image? How strong were your beliefs? As you affirm a statement it merges into your consciousness and becomes accepted as your belief. Eventually, a new reality emerges based on that statement. There are no accidents you experience what you think about. Look back through your assessment to see if you have experienced what you thought about. Daily self-talk and visualizations are habits acquired over time. It is an ongoing process requiring daily attention and action. Your self-talk can build or tear down the image you have of yourself.

Meaningful affirmations create a sense of identity. Notice the immense power words and language have on performance and behavior. Listen to your self-talk. Self-talk heightens your stature to achieve your desired dreams. As you make strides edit your script to make it consistent with your new goals. Notice how you think with words and exactly what words trigger your pictures. As others are talking to you keep talking to yourself.

Take action to set goals and deadlines. Then apply hard work. Be disciplined and consistent as you set out to solve a problem or find an opportunity. Apply passion to your purpose. Continue on your path to a meaningful purpose. Being and doing leads to results of having. Remember to give thanks.

Master your mental game

Inner knowing comes in different ways, but you know it when it comes from a voice deep within you. Understanding causes a paradigm shift that develops trust. The more confident you are in knowing, the easier it will be to produce your desired result.

Deep within the initial question lingers, "Can I do this?" Conquering each challenge develops your trust to answer that question. Each obstacle that you overcome peels away another layer, like an onion. This gets you closer to the center of your being, where ultimately you discover the authentic you and the answer, "Yes I can." Then you face the next challenge, where you find another layer to peel and start all over again, peeling another layer and conquering new doubts, but in the end you find more meaning.

The more balanced you are, the firmer you will be committed and less drama will distract you from your pursuit. You begin to see improvements in all areas of your life, including family and relationships, business and finances, health, happiness and well-being.

Passion at the point of execution creates magic

Accuracy and precision added to passion in executing is a winning combination that leads to better performance, increased productivity, and more favorable results.

Execution in golf is the point at which your swing causes the club to collide with the ball. Impact is the point when you need the most concentration and power. In the same way, your carefully focused actions in business explode a vision into a reality. In business your signature on the dotted line of a contract represents the execution. After executing a contract in business the negotiating ends. Therefore, a wise strategy in business and in golf is to do a thorough assessment before you execute.

After you execute your energy shifts to focus on the follow through. How well you negotiate and how precisely you execute determine how much effort is needed for the follow through. A better assessment leads to greater clarity and less conflict. Executing with precision creates successful results and brings in the dough either at the flag on the golf course or after your performance under the contract.

The putting green is the last stretch of the execution where the ball rolls into the hole and the score of each hole is registered. This is where the cash register rings. Without precision in your execution, you may wish for a mulligan to improve your performance on a replay. Only golf's mulligan gives you that opportunity to replay a bad shot. If you treat each hole on the golf course like a major deal in business, the objective of your strategic plan, where you either succeed or fail, the golf course, gives you at least eighteen attempts to execute successfully. Business does not allow you to say, "I'll take that play over." A failure in business may wipe you out. Execute from a well-centered position to prevent the need for a mulligan. Don't count on replaying a bad shot.

Strive for mastery

Mastery is doing what you love, doing it best, and always doing it. Mastery is the right combination of passion, extensive knowledge, constantly practicing proper techniques, and refined skills. By involving yourself more with what generates passion in your life, small victories begin to build. A most rewarding experience is that of mastering your skill. You gain gratification, mobilization of your spirit, enjoyment of the challenge, authority to lead, and recognition.

Mastery is the enhancement of your skills to such a level that you experience an intimate relationship with nature - one of the most powerful experiences you can have. Mastery demands determination, focus, and concentration. Like the eye of a tiger focusing on executing with precision, the mind of a master is intent on achievement, with every ounce of energy aligned toward devouring the target.

Even for a master, when your emotional life is off-center it affects your performance. Precision is not perfection. Practicing for perfection is a setup for frustration because impossible goals unnecessarily utilize your energy. Precision, however, is an achievable goal. Likewise, mastery is not an end target but a goal to strive toward constantly with excellence and precision.

When you are striving for mastery, there is no room for the ego. One of your hardest lessons will be when you encounter yourself. It takes mental maturity but may be necessary to un-invite your ego as an unwelcomed visitor on your mission for mastery. That experience of firing your employees will come in handy when you attempt to get rid of your ego.

Practice your craft with such passion that mastery becomes your measure of accomplishment. When a thirst urges you to study more, become better, or practice incessantly, you will know that you are on a path seeking excellence, which ultimately leads toward mastery. A solid foundation of skill is built through perseverance and practice. Patience is a virtue of those seeking mastery. Management of inner emotions aligned with continual practice of proper skills enhances your performance to a masterful level.

Mastery gives you authority to dominate

The move toward mastery brings power. Humbly accept your natural abilities for transformation to occur. Mastery is reserved for a few deserving leaders who have learned there are no shortcuts. Mastery strips you of the superficial and takes you to the height of your game. While power, money or influence may appear to override a lack of basic skills, mastery never gives such an illusion. Mastery is the result after consistently applying tenacious persistence and weathering torrential storms. Accept your failures as a part of success, and keep practicing and executing your game plan with determination and faith that eventually brings respect and domination. Believing anything is possible you will eventually find yourself in Wonderland, being recognized for achieving your dream.

LINK # 9

LEAVE FOOTPRINTS IN THE SAND

Interaction at the 19th hole

"After we finish, we'll meet at the 19th hole," I hear one of my golf partners say. At the end of the 18th hole, I hang around the cart, waiting for the rest of the foursome to go to the next hole. Some golfers disappear into the clubhouse lounge. I take the cart to look for the 19th hole. After some frustration, I arrive back at the first hole. Eventually, I give up and go into the lounge. My teammates are enjoying snacks and drinks. When I ask about the 19th hole, they all look at me, but only one responds: "The 19th hole is the most important part of the golf course."

My golf lessons taught about specific setup positions, degrees of loft on the club face, and body movements, the 19th hole was never mentioned. I later learn that the 19th hole does not exist, but indeed it is the most important part of the course. The 19th hole is where relationships are leveraged. The bond that we started forging on the golf course is solidified at the 19th hole. It is not necessary to influence the masses, only one important person. That is the importance of networking after the game at the watering hole, known within golf circles as the 19th hole.

At the 19th hole you meet people from all areas of the globe. The common denominator is golf. At the 19th hole, your handicap does not matter. Only trust matters—the kind of trust that joins partnerships. The 19th hole is where golfers become partners during camaraderie. The common language spoken is that of bonding relationships, doing deals, and making money.

"Before people do business with you, they must know and like you," the starter had told me.

At the 19th hole, resourceful alliances are formed, not by force but through influence that optimizes potential for long-term success. Relationships formed at the 19th hole lead to major success. They encourage inclusion rather than exclusion. They are expansive rather than limiting; they empower rather than deplete.

Golf lessons and practice teach you how to balance and be flexible to improve your skill. Lessons do not teach the importance of the 19th hole. That you learn through experience and bonding. Finding your right stance gives you the leverage to strengthen your swing. You practice bonding the same way you practice your swing. Aim towards executing bonding relationships with accuracy and precision.

Leverage your network and support systems

The 19th hole allows you to connect with people who can assist your business venture. People skills are especially necessary to leverage relationships. What one person cannot do alone, can be done by building on the backs of others through team effort.

Leveraging relationships results from bonding and supportive relationships developed over the long term that give people the foundation necessary to excel to great heights, recover or climb out of any rough. This also builds togetherness and mutual respect within communities. The 19th hole is also where celebration takes place; celebration that maintains the relationship and keeps it joyfully bonded. Leveraging relationships at the 19th hole allows celebration whether you win or lose. Exponential leveraging is when both you and your customers move to a new level of success. Imagine creating a successful 19th hole with your team, leaving footprints that impact around the globe.

Leverage requires leaps of faith. The first key in bonding is being authentic. That can be frightening. Before bonding takes place with another you learn to gently open up to yourself, to listen internally and become aware of your inner voice. The tranquility of a golf course adds to provide an opportunity to listen to another, communicate, and bond. These experiences with partners and clients week after week prepare you to join in alliances and joint ventures with those who have similar rhythm and styles and create supportive, dynamic teams that emerge through challenges and excel beyond ordinary success.

The insights in this book encourage you to search for that crossroad where your parents' paths connect. Finding it forces you to acknowledge the ingredients from your parents that are still baking within you. Completion in that baking process allows you to move towards your greatness, pursue your path with passion and unwavering confidence. Through powerful insights, you quickly see measurable results in your life and your business.

Searching to find your path to a meaningful pursuit is itself a meaningful pursuit. Life is a rose garden. Expect thorns along the way. Do not let the short-lived pain turn you around from the life-long happiness that you gain in discovering you.

* * *

www.ingramcontent.com/pod-product-compliance
Lightning Source LLC
Chambersburg PA
CBHW051528170526
45165CB00002B/658